W9-CAM-089

HABITS
of a
Godly Woman

JOYCE MEYER

New York • Nashville

FaithWords
Hachette Book Group
1290 Avenue of the Americas, New York, NY 10104
faithwords.com
twitter.com/faithwords

First Edition: June 2020

FaithWords is a division of Hachette Book Group, Inc.

The FaithWords name and logo are trademarks of Hachette Book Group, Inc.

The publisher is not responsible for websites (or their content) that are not owned by the publisher.

The Hachette Speakers Bureau provides a wide range of authors for speaking events. To find out more, go to www.hachettespeakersbureau.com or call (866) 376–6591.

Library of Congress Cataloging-in-Publication Data has been applied for.

ISBNs: 978–1-5460–1349–5 (paper over board), 978–1-5460–1347–1 (ebook), 978–1-5460–1740–0 (international)

Printed in the United States of America
LSC-C

Contents

INTRODUCTION

If you change your habits, you'll change your life.
That may sound like a bold statement, but I
believe it's true. To a great degree, your life con-
sists of your habits—the things you think, say,
and do repeatedly. The way you spend your
time, your money, and your energy each day
is largely based on habits. If you're like most
people, you have some kind of routine for every
day. Even if the daily routine varies, you may
have a routine for each week—certain things
you want to do and certain things you have to
do. Over time, those things have become habits for you.

All kinds of habits are at work in our physical lives, sometimes without our even realizing
it. We have a habit of going to work, a habit of

brushing our teeth, a habit of seeing the doctor for an annual physical, a habit of taking out the trash on certain days of the week, habits for cooking and cleaning at home, and habits with friends and family. We may also have habits regarding exercise or lack of exercise, or habits pertaining to the amount of time we spend watching television or looking at the screen of an electronic device.

We also have habits in our minds. We may have positive mental attitudes and thought patterns that cause us to be confident in everything we do. Or we may have habits of negative thinking that make everything feel like a chore. We may have ways of thinking about resources, such as money or time, that allow us to use them wisely, or ways of thinking that keep us continually in debt or stressed because we're running late.

In addition to our physical and mental habits, we also have many emotional habits. We

may be in the habit of feeling sorry for ourselves when we don't get what we want. We
may have a habit of becoming fearful when we
hear thunder and see lightning. An emotional
habit of anger or judgment toward a certain
person may be ingrained in us. Or, when we
see people who are obviously needy or struggling in life, we may have a habit of feeling
compassion and reaching out to help them.

The habits I have mentioned are only a few
of the habits that determine how we live our
lives. I'm sure, if you stop and think about it,
you could identify a lot of habits you live by.
Some of those habits would be good, such as
keeping your car clean, using coupons to save
money at the grocery store, or visiting someone in a nursing home each week, and some
would be ones you'd like to change, such as
biting your nails, drinking too much caffeine,
or being easily frustrated. The good news
about habits you'd like to break is that they

can always be changed! Every day you live, you have a chance to develop a new habit or to break a bad one and replace it with a good one.

When I hear women talk about their habits, they usually don't mention their good ones, but they do talk about wanting to change their bad ones. I've never met anyone who didn't have some good habits, but I've also never met a woman who didn't have other habits she would like to change. All of us have a mixture of good habits and not-so-good ones, so we all have room to improve.

In this book, I don't simply want to talk about changing habits, though you will read a lot about that. I also want to specifically explore with you the habits of a godly woman—not just any woman, but one who wants to keep growing in God and live every aspect of her life as He would have her to live it. The book doesn't address every single habit of a godly woman, but it does focus on some that are most important and that will help you go far as you seek to become a more godly woman.

Many adjectives can describe a woman. She can be successful. She can be beautiful. She can be smart. She can be a talented artist or singer or homemaker. She can be gifted in all kinds of ways and have lots of different attributes. But the best quality for any woman to have is godliness. I believe a godly woman is someone who is confident, peaceful, and enjoys life. She has developed habits that make her like Christ in her behavior, and she delights in continuing to grow in Him. She represents Him well everywhere she goes and is a blessing to everyone she comes in contact with.

Becoming a godly woman is a process. It doesn't happen overnight. The apostle Paul says we "are being transformed into his image with ever-increasing glory" (2 Cor. 3:18), which is a New Testament way of saying that God keeps changing us, continually taking us from one level of spiritual maturity to the next. One way to be disciplined and diligent about our spiritual growth is to purposefully develop habits that will help us become more and more godly. Instead of spending our time trying to break habits, I suggest focusing on making good habits. Focusing our energy in positive directions is usually a better path to change than continually focusing on our weaknesses, which can cause us to lose heart and remain stuck in the very habits we most need to eliminate. Through staying focused on positive change, we move toward becoming the people God wants us to be, and we get to experience the joy and sense of purpose that comes with fulfilling His plans and purposes for our lives.

God's desire is for you and me to be "conformed to the image of his Son" (Rom. 8:29). When I first read this verse, I read it in the

Amplified Bible, Classic Edition, which helped me understand that being conformed to the image of Christ is to "share inwardly His likeness." God is ready and willing to help us become more like Jesus by the power of the Holy Spirit, but He won't do it all for us. We need to be obedient to His direction and work with the Holy Spirit to develop godly habits. I've written this book to help you do that.

At the end of each chapter, you'll find a list of three or four Scripture references under the heading "Habit Builders." These Bible verses and passages will help you know what God's Word says about each habit and support you as you integrate each practice into your life. Experts say that developing a new habit or replacing a bad habit with a good one can take twenty-one to thirty days, so you can expect the development of godly habits to be a journey. It will take time to develop each habit, but once it becomes part of your life, you won't have to build it again; you'll simply need to maintain it.

When you reach the end of the book and have read about the various habits of a godly woman, you'll find some helpful encouragement and advice on practical steps you can take to develop and strengthen the habits you'd like to see in your life. I'm happy to be able to share these insights with you, and I pray you will find this book valuable as you continue to become the woman God has created you to be.

CHAPTER 1

A Role Model for a Godly Woman

Oh, to have a church built up with the deep godliness of people who know the Lord in their very hearts, and will seek to follow the Lamb wherever he goes!

—Charles Spurgeon

For years, people have thought of the woman described in Proverbs 31:10–30 as the kind of person Christian women should aspire to be. You can find greeting cards, wall art, decorative plates, coffee cups, T-shirts, and other items with this passage printed on them because so many women know someone who exemplifies this woman's traits and so many want the words that describe her to apply to them. Many obituaries and funeral services include these words because people feel they are appropriate for godly women who have lived exemplary lives.

We don't want to make the mistake of being legalistic in our understanding of the qualities of the Proverbs 31 woman. While her habits and practices provide great examples for us, God made each one of us to be unique. Because it is often our very uniqueness that equips us to do and be all He has planned for us, we want to be careful to emulate the habits of the Proverbs 31 woman in ways that are authentic, not legalistic or rigid. This is why the guidance of the Holy Spirit is so important to this process. We aren't striving to become like

> *We aren't striving to become like someone else but prayerfully seeking to become the fullest expression of who God intended each one of us to be.*

someone else; we are prayerfully seeking to become the fullest expression of who God intended each one of us to be. Nevertheless, the Proverbs 31 woman definitely demonstrates many qualities of a godly woman, and for that reason, I want to start this book by looking closely at the way she lives her life.

An excellent woman [one who is spiritual, capable, intelligent, and virtuous], who is he who can find her? Her value is more precious than jewels *and* her worth is far above rubies *or* pearls.

The heart of her husband trusts in her [with secure confidence], and he will have no lack of gain.

She comforts, encourages, *and* does him only good and not evil all the days of her life.

She looks for wool and flax and works with willing hands in delight.

She is like the merchant ships [abounding with treasure]; she brings her [household's] food from far away.

She rises while it is still night and gives food to her household and assigns tasks to her maids.

She considers a field before she buys or accepts it [expanding her business prudently]; with her profits she plants fruitful vines in her vineyard.

She equips herself with strength [spiritual, mental, and physical fitness for her God-given task] and makes her arms strong.

She sees that her gain is good; her lamp does not go out, but it burns continually through the night [she is prepared for whatever lies ahead].

She stretches out her hand to the distaff, and her hands hold the spindle [as she spins wool into thread for clothing].

She opens *and* extends her hand to the poor, and she reaches out her filled hands to the needy.

She does not fear the snow for her household, for all in her household are clothed in [expensive] scarlet [wool].

She makes for herself coverlets, cushions, *and* rugs of tapestry. Her clothing is linen, pure *and* fine, and purple [wool].

Her husband is known in the [city's] gates, when he sits among the elders of the land.

She makes [fine] linen garments and sells them; and supplies sashes to the merchants.

Strength and dignity are her clothing *and* her position is strong and secure; and she smiles at the future [knowing that she and her family are prepared].

She opens her mouth in [skillful and godly] wisdom, and the teaching of kindness is on her tongue [giving counsel and instruction].

She looks well to how things go in her household, and does not eat the bread of idleness.

Her children rise up and call her blessed (happy, prosperous, to be admired); her husband also, and he praises her, *saying*, "Many daughters have done nobly, *and* well [with the strength of character that is steadfast in goodness], but you excel them all."

Charm *and* grace are deceptive, and [superficial] beauty is vain, but a woman who fears the LORD [reverently worshiping, obeying, serving, and trusting Him with awe-filled respect], she shall be praised. (Prov. 31:10–30 AMP)

I hope you'll take time to read these words more than once and think about yourself and your life. You'll probably see some characteristics of the godly woman that you think describe you fairly accurately and recognize some things that she did well and that you do well, too. As you read about her, you may also realize that you want to improve in certain ways, and you may find areas in which you do not excel.

Part of growing as a godly woman means building on what you're already good at and improving in areas that are not your greatest strengths. It also involves knowing yourself well enough to recognize what your strengths and weaknesses are. I have a friend who absolutely is not a good cook. She doesn't like cooking, has no desire to like it, and doesn't do it. So, either her husband cooks or they order carryout, and that is okay. Part of being a godly woman is embracing your uniqueness and feeling no shame if you aren't like other women you know.

Throughout this book, you'll recognize that some of the habits that will help you grow in godliness are mentioned in Proverbs 31. For example, there's a verse on excellence, one on serving others, one on discipline, and one on generosity. All of these describe the godly woman.

A godly woman possesses great strength and is a blessing everywhere she goes. I believe this is what you want for yourself and what God wants for you. You can count on Him to help you!

Habit Builders

Do not conform to the pattern of this world, but be transformed by the renewing of your mind. Then you will be able to test and approve what God's will is—his good, pleasing and perfect will.

Romans 12:2

Therefore, if anyone is in Christ,
the new creation has come:
The old has gone, the new is here!

2 Corinthians 5:17

Do not love the world or anything
in the world. If anyone loves the world,
love for the Father is not in them.
For everything in the world—the lust
of the flesh, the lust of the eyes,
and the pride of life—comes not
from the Father but from the world.

1 John 2:15–16

CHAPTER 2

The Habit of God's Word

When you read God's Word, you must constantly be saying to yourself, "It is talking to me, and about me."

—Søren Kierkegaard

People today are desperate for truth, direction, wisdom, and peace. I have observed this to be the case for people of all ages and from a variety of life experiences. Sadly, I have also seen many people chasing after these things in ways that will never satisfy them. We all have so much information bombarding our minds that it can be extremely difficult to determine which claims and promises to trust.

The fact that you are reading this book suggests that you are a woman who is hungry for trustworthy truth, direction, wisdom, and peace. There's only one totally reliable source—and it's absolutely trustworthy. It's God's Word, the Bible. One of the best habits you can develop is the habit of knowing and studying God's Word on a regular basis. This habit is essential for any godly woman, and it is also a practice that will bless and encourage you each day.

Many women struggle with keeping their priorities straight. So many things compete for our energy and

> *One of the best habits you can develop is the habit of knowing and studying God's Word on a regular basis.*

attention—caring for family, being a good employee, managing job stress, spending time

with friends, fulfilling church and community responsibilities, grocery shopping, bill
paying, and other duties involved in running
a household. On top of all of that, sometimes
we'd just like to sit on the couch and watch
a movie without interruption. We'd appreciate a few moments to prioritize self-care. This
isn't a book about priorities, so I won't spend
any more time on this subject except to say
this: If you make God's Word a priority, everything else will fall into place. You may have to
restructure certain commitments or adjust your
schedule in some ways, but putting God's Word
first in your life will bring you strength, clarity,
peace, and guidance like nothing else you can
spend your time doing.

I have said this many times, but I want to
repeat it here: God's Word is very precious. *It
is worth prioritizing*, even if you have to get up
thirty minutes earlier than you already do. I
can truly say that I love His Word, and that it

has changed me and changed my life as nothing else could have ever done. I've also seen it bring miraculous changes to the lives of other people. I could speak for hours about how powerful and how wonderful the Word of God is and never grow tired of talking about it. If I could give only one piece of advice to every woman I know, I would say that after being saved, the most important thing anyone can ever do is to study, meditate on, and obey God's Word. There are many ways available for us to take in the Word of God. We can read and study the Bible or books about biblical topics that may help us understand the Scriptures more clearly. We also have teachings available to us through other forms of media, including television, the Internet, radio, and other sources.

Although on the surface the Bible looks like many other books, it is completely unique in both its essence and its impact. God's words are living words, filled with life and power. The power of God is actually inherent in His words, and it saves us, heals us, sets us free, leads and guides us, comforts us, corrects us, and encourages us. Second Timothy 3:16 says, "All Scripture is God-breathed." We can't say that about any other book on earth. The words of Scripture are not words that come from human intellect or words based on human experience. They are words that impart God's life and truth to us.

Many people have not been taught about the Bible. They may know various Bible stories and be aware of certain biblical principles, but they do not realize how powerful God's Word can be in their lives. They do not know that it can be a lamp to their feet and a light to their path (Ps. 119:105) or understand that it contains the answer to every question and the solution to every problem or need they may face. Others know about the Bible, but because their exposure to its truth and power has been limited, they are unaware that it contains the answers they desperately need.

I know this from personal experience. For many years, I attended a church that provided me with a great biblical foundation for salvation, but I learned very little beyond that. I had many problems in my life, and God's Word could have helped me with them. However, I wasn't learning how to read and understand it in such a way that I

> *The power of God is actually inherent in His words, and it saves us, heals us, sets us free, leads and guides us, comforts us, corrects us, and encourages us.*

could gain victory over any of my challenges. I certainly didn't know how to pursue the peace I so desperately wanted, and I didn't realize I could find it in God's Word.

I was not taught to study the Bible for myself, and because I didn't know God's Word,

I was not aware of the many deceptions in the world that can mislead us. For example, before I worked in ministry, I worked at an office where a coworker studied astrology. She sincerely believed that the position of the planets and stars directed her life, and she used astrology to help her make decisions. At the time, the things she talked about seemed to make sense and were intriguing to me. Since I did not know that the Bible teaches that consulting the stars for guidance is wrong (Rev. 21:8), I was ripe for the devil's deception. The things she talked about caught my attention, but, thank God, He kept me from getting involved in them.

People can easily make costly mistakes in many areas of life (as my coworker who consulted the stars did) if they do not know that God's Word can teach them how to think and act in every situation. If they live according to His Word, giving it priority over every other source of information, they will find the peace, joy, and fulfillment in life they're looking for.

We should always respect and honor God's Word and give it a place of priority in every situation in our lives. His Word will help us when nothing else will.

Whether you have been living as a godly woman for years or you just became a Christian yesterday, God's Word has so much to offer you. The first step toward growing in godliness is to develop the habit of studying His Word. Know it, read it, meditate on its truths (roll them over and over in your mind, thinking about them deeply), and apply it to your life. Consider setting aside time in the morning or at some other point during the day to read your Bible, study it, and pray about what you learn from it. You might also use resources such as a concordance, a commentary, a study Bible, or a Bible dictionary to help you understand the Scriptures. In addition, there are many books and teachings available to help you study and live by God's Word.

The Holy Spirit is your Helper, and He will lead you into truth. Ask Him to make God's Word alive to you and to cause you to fall in love with it. Make it more important to you than anything else, and you will experience amazing spiritual growth and a quality of life you've never known before.

Habit Builders

As for God, his way is perfect:
the LORD's word is flawless;
he shields all who take refuge in him.

Psalm 18:30

All Scripture is God-breathed and
is useful for teaching, rebuking, correcting
and training in righteousness,

so that the servant of God
may be thoroughly equipped
for every good work.

2 Timothy 3:16–17

For the word of God is alive and active.
Sharper than any double-edged sword,
it penetrates even to dividing soul
and spirit, joints and marrow; it judges
the thoughts and attitudes of the heart.

Hebrews 4:12

CHAPTER 3

The Habit of God's Presence

Draw near to God and He will draw near to you.

—James 4:8 NKJV

The best habits a godly woman can develop are spiritual habits—prayer, worship, studying and obeying God's Word, and simply spending time in God's presence, focused on Him. Of course, women with full lives have lots of other things to do too, but if we build our lives on our spiritual habits, everything else in our lives will go much better. Jesus said in Matthew 6:33, "But seek first his kingdom and his righteousness, and all these things will be given to you as well." The word *his* in this verse refers to God, so the passage is saying that if we seek God's kingdom and if we seek right relationship with Him above everything else, we can trust Him to bring us the other things we need.

The enemy knows that our lives are often stressful and filled with pressing responsibilities that compete for our attention, and he uses those pressures to try to convince us that we simply do not have time to spend with God or to study the Bible. He knows that if he can keep us out of God's presence, we will be powerless, unprotected, dissatisfied, and in a constant state of confusion and frustration.

Early in my Christian walk, I fell for the enemy's deceptions for a time, and I experienced the disappointment of living a powerless and unfulfilled life. I could sense my spiritual hunger, and I finally understood that I needed

God's presence more than anything else. As I began spending time with Him, I discovered that He longed to spend time with me, developing an intimate relationship that would restore my soul and give my life new meaning.

One of the greatest benefits of taking time to focus on God's presence is an inner sense of peace, joy, contentment, unconditional love, and being led by the Holy Spirit—a deep, lasting satisfaction that cannot be found in any other source. Unfortunately, there are many women—even Christian women—who try to find fulfillment in a variety of other places. They pursue worldly things—money, promotions, positions, and relationships—hoping to find the happiness that eludes them. I did this for a number of years when I first started walking with the Lord, but when I became tired of living a powerless life, I cried out to God for help.

That's when God began to teach me that I

needed to put Him *first*. He led me to several Scriptures, including Psalm 91:1–2, which says, "He who dwells in the secret place of the Most High shall remain stable *and* fixed under the shadow of the Almighty [Whose power no foe can withstand]. I will say of the Lord, He is my Refuge and my Fortress, my God; on Him I lean *and* rely, *and* in Him I [confidently] trust!" (AMPC). In other words, when we spend time with God, we learn how to dwell in the secret place of His presence. And as we do, we experience an unshakable stability full of peace, power, and protection.

It is important to remember that doing things *for* God does not replace spending time *with* Him. You may serve on church committees, sing in the choir, lead

> *One of the greatest benefits of taking time to focus on God's presence is an inner sense of peace, joy, contentment, unconditional love, and being led by the Holy Spirit.*

a small group, or volunteer to teach vacation Bible school, but none of these activities can take the place of spending personal time with God.

God longs to have an intimate relationship with you. What an awesome opportunity you have to spend time in the very presence of almighty God! It is a privilege not to be taken lightly. If you want to have a close, intimate relationship with the Father and reap the benefits of being in His presence, you can. But to enjoy that kind of walk with Him, you'll need to be willing to regularly schedule time to be alone with Him.

> *It is important to remember that doing things for God does not replace spending time with Him.*

For me, the best time to spend time with God is first thing in the morning, before I get so distracted with other things that it takes me two or three hours to unwind and calm down enough to hear from

Him. I'm not saying that your time with God must be in the morning, but it is important to give God a portion of the *best* part of your day, not the worst. I believe that as we give God the "first fruits" of our best time instead of our "leftovers," He multiplies our remaining time, so we can accomplish all that we need to do and do it with joy.

When we spend time in God's presence, we may use that time to read, study, memorize, and meditate on Scripture. This will help us better understand God's character and, at the same time, renew our minds with the truth. By reading the Word, we are actually having fellowship with God, because the Word *is* God (John 1:1).

Prayer is also an important part of spending time in God's presence. The next chapter of this book focuses exclusively on prayer, so you can read more about it there, but for now let me simply say that prayer is not just about us talking to God; it is also about His talking to us. Once we have spent time in praise and worship to Him and have shared the needs and desires of our hearts, we need to be silent so we can hear Him speak to our hearts. Often He will answer us by reminding us of a Bible verse. Sometimes He answers by flooding our soul with peace. Sometimes we simply have an inner knowing about what we are to do or which direction we should take. The way God chooses to speak to us is up to Him. All we need to do is give Him the *time* and *opportunity* to do so.

God cares about you and longs to have a more intimate relationship with you. I can't urge you strongly enough to spend time with Him every day. Nothing and no one else can provide the wisdom, direction, power, protection, joy, comfort, encouragement, advice, and peace that every woman needs. If you long for a deeply personal, fulfilling relationship with

God and a more powerful, meaningful life, it will require an investment of your time. But I can tell you from experience that the investment pays huge benefits. God loves you very much and longs to spend time with you today. Don't keep Him waiting.

Habit Builders

The LORD himself goes before you
and will be with you; he will never
leave you nor forsake you.
Do not be afraid; do not be discouraged.

Deuteronomy 31:8

You make known to me the path
of life; you will fill me with joy in
your presence, with eternal pleasures
at your right hand.

Psalm 16:11

Where can I go from your Spirit?
Where can I flee from your presence?
If I go up to the heavens, you are there;
if I make my bed in the depths,
you are there. If I rise on the wings
of the dawn, if I settle on the far side of the
sea, even there your hand will guide me,
your right hand will hold me fast.

Psalm 139:7–10

And I will ask the Father, and he will
give you another advocate to help you
and be with you forever.

John 14:16

CHAPTER 4

The Habit of Prayer

Prayer is where the action is.

—John Wesley

Developing the habit of prayer is essential for a godly woman. When I mention "developing the habit of prayer," what comes to mind for you? Do you think of a pastor saying a prayer during a service while a congregation sits quietly with their heads bowed or a minister leading a group of people in the Lord's Prayer on Sundays? Do you think of someone kneeling beside their bed at the end of the day? Do you think of someone known as an intercessor praying for hours in a room called a "prayer closet"? Or do you think of a family gathered around a table to say grace before a meal?

Praying, as expressed in the examples above, is a practice. However, it is also much more than a ritual. Prayer is direct communication with God, and like Him, authentic prayer is not bound by religious traditions or regulations. Prayer does not have to happen in a certain place or at a specific time; it can happen anywhere, anytime. It does not have to follow any rules. It simply comes from the heart, and when you pray, nothing that concerns you is off-limits.

It is a wonderful thing that prayer is so boundless, because the world doesn't stop so we can pursue our heartfelt desire to become godly women. We have to engage in the habits of godliness in the midst of real life, which includes things that compete for our time and energy.

I have great news about developing the habit of prayer while also living an active life: It just may be the simplest of all godly habits to form. I remember when God began teaching me to pray. Perhaps the biggest surprise to me was that prayer is not complicated. God wants praying to be enjoyable and to feel natural for us. He wants us to pray heartfelt prayers and to be completely honest with Him about how we feel. He wants us to talk with Him and hear from Him as we would during a conversation with our best friend. He wants prayer to be an integral part of our everyday lives—and to be the most powerful yet the easiest thing we do each day.

> *We have to engage in the habits of godliness in the midst of real life, which includes things that compete for our time and energy.*

Anytime we direct a thought toward God, that's prayer. Consider your life. How many times have you been to the grocery store and been shocked at the price of eggs or milk? Many women have that kind of experience and think, *Money is already tight for us, and now these basic things we need are getting more and more expensive. We really need You, God, to help us in our finances.* Or maybe you have a child who is really struggling to grasp certain concepts in school, and that is causing trouble. When you see her getting frustrated with homework, you think, *Oh, God, help her understand this!* When you see a car accident and realize it could have happened to you had you left home one minute sooner, you may think, *Thank You, God, that I ran late today!* Thoughts like these, which come to you so naturally, are actually prayers. And they are just as powerful as any other type of prayer. Effective prayer doesn't depend on where you pray or how long you pray or whether you say certain spiritual-sounding phrases or eloquent speech. All it takes to pray is a heart that is open to and communicates with God.

I hope you feel relieved and encouraged to know that prayer is not something you have to add to your daily to-do list or calendar, nor is it something you have to go to church to do. Having said that, let me also say that I do believe that having a specific time set aside for prayer each day is beneficial. Some people are called to spend several hours praying every day, but that is not a rule for everyone. God leads each person to the kind of prayer life He knows they need, and the person who spends two or three hours alone praying is not necessarily closer to God or a "better Christian" than the one who prays one-sentence prayers multiple times throughout each day. The point of prayer is to ask God to turn our hearts toward Him and to ask Him to work in our lives. He responds to sincere requests, whatever form they take. We can ask God for anything and everything we need and desire. James 4:2 says that there are things we do not have because we do not ask God for them. He wants to hear our requests.

Prayer opens the door for God to work. When we pray, we partner with Him in the spiritual realm, and then things happen in the natural realm.

Developing the habit of prayer is about learning to communicate with God about everything in life, remembering that He is always with you, and asking for His help and guidance in every situation. You can say a prayer in a few seconds, and it's very easy to do. Most importantly, it's powerful.

> Prayer opens the door for God to work.
> When we pray, we partner with Him in the spiritual realm, and then things happen in the natural realm.

One sentence, a phrase, or just one word—if it's an earnest prayer—can change everything. It can make your day better instead of worse; it can cause you to make a good decision instead of a bad one; it can keep you from saying something you shouldn't or lead you to say something that is very helpful. The Amplified Bible's translation of James 5:16 has encouraged me greatly in my prayer life, and I believe it will encourage you, too: "The heartfelt and persistent prayer of a righteous man (believer) can accomplish much [when put into action and made effective by God—it is dynamic and can have tremendous power]."

As you grow as a godly woman and as you go through various seasons of your life, your prayer habits will probably change. Ten years from now you may have more free time than you do today, and you may want to spend more time in focused prayer than your schedule currently allows. By then, you may enjoy praying so much that you find yourself praying for an hour or two without even paying attention to the clock. My encouragement to you is simple: Recognize that even short, simple prayers are effective; realize that prayer is what brings God's power into every situation you face; and make prayer a part of every day you live. Whether you pray a little or pray a lot, just get into the habit of talking to God about everything in your life and listening for Him to answer you.

Habit Builders

Be joyful in hope, patient in affliction,
faithful in prayer.

Romans 12:12

And pray in the Spirit on all occasions
with all kinds of prayers and requests.
With this in mind, be alert and always
keep on praying for all the Lord's people.

Ephesians 6:18

Let us then approach God's throne
of grace with confidence, so that we
may receive mercy and find grace
to help us in our time of need.

Hebrews 4:16

CHAPTER 5
The Habit of Faith

Faith is not belief without proof, but trust without reservation.

—D. Elton Trueblood

If there's anything that can keep a godly woman from developing the habit of faith, it's fear. Most of us struggle with fear—anything from a debilitating fear, such as fear of flying that keeps us from traveling to see the world or visit loved ones, to general anxiety or nervousness or a tendency to worry. Fear is a tactic the devil uses to hinder our faith and keep us from living in God's will for our lives. If the enemy can trap us in fear, he can keep us from moving forward into all that God has for us. But we don't have to fall prey to his evil devices.

The first step to overcoming fear is to recognize its source. The Bible tells us that "the Spirit God gave us does not make us timid, but gives us power, love and self-discipline" (2 Tim. 1:7). The Bible also tells us that God's perfect love for us is incompatible with fear: "But perfect love drives out fear, because fear has to do with punishment" (1 John 4:18).

The Bible includes many passages urging us not to be afraid (Josh. 1:9; Isa. 41:10; Isa. 43:1; John 14:27). When we read stories in the Bible about people God used to any degree, we see that He said to them over and over, "Do not fear" (Gen. 15:1; Num. 21:34; Josh. 1:9; Dan. 10:12; Matt. 14:27).

Fear is a feeling that can create reactions in our physical bodies. It may cause us to tremble, turn red, sweat, or have shaky knees. But the Bible doesn't say, "Sweat not," "Tremble not," or "Shake not"—it says, "Fear not!"

The Greek word for *fear* implies "flight" or "running away from something." When the Bible says, "Fear not," it doesn't mean, "Don't *feel* fear." God is saying, "When fear comes, don't run away. Don't let it stop you from going forward."

Even though I am a very bold person now, there was a time when I wasn't walking in the confidence and blessings God had for me. My early years were rooted in fear. The spirit of fear was my constant companion. A variety of fears invaded my thoughts on a regular basis, including the fear of harm, fear of rejection, fear of other people, fear of the future, fear of people knowing I was being abused, fear of never being loved, and fear that my life was ruined. But through the years, God has helped me understand how the bondage of fear took hold in my life, and He has shown me how to be free from fear's torment.

The best way to overcome fear is with faith. The enemy will send thoughts of fear against us, but we can choose whether to agree with them and focus on them or not. Through the power of faith, we can resist Satan's attacks of fear. Faith is a force that draws the will of God into our lives. In order for fearful mindsets to be broken

> *The best way to overcome fear is with faith.*

and for us to live in freedom, our thinking needs to be renewed and charged with faith. Hebrews 11:6 says, "Without faith it is impossible to please God."

Would you say you are filled with faith? Or does the enemy torment you with fear? Does he harass you often with feelings of anxiety or keep you nervous or worried about various things? I believe that many women experience all kinds of fears and worries, but those who choose to refuse Satan's lies and have faith in God's Word overcome fear and thwart the devil's plan to paralyze them and keep them from becoming the mighty women of God that He planned for them to be.

Early in my walk with God, I recognized that fear played a big role in my life. I made a conscious decision to stand against fear and to deliberately stop thinking fearful thoughts and speaking fear-filled words. Although that decision made no sense to my mind and my *feelings* didn't back it up at the time, I chose to believe God and build my faith upon His Word.

But something was still missing. So I prayed and said, "I don't see very much changing in my life, even though I have done what You led me to do. I have stopped thinking and speaking fearful and negative thoughts, so what's going on?" His response was so clear. God helped me see that I had *stopped* thinking and speaking fearful and negative things, but I had not *started* saying positive, faith-filled things.

I learned that it is not enough to stop doing the wrong thing—we also need to start doing the right thing. In other words, we overcome our old habits by developing new ones. In my journey to freedom from fear, the right thing was to begin speaking the promises of God, which are recorded for everyone in His Word.

Genesis 1 tells us that God spoke and created the world and everything in it. Romans 4:17 says we serve a God who "speaks of the nonexistent things that [He has foretold and promised] as if they [already] existed" (AMPC). With this in mind, I made a list of confessions—things I declare aloud that are all based on God's Word. Two or three times a day I would speak these truths over my life.

When God first called me, He put a dream in my heart that one day I would have a world-wide ministry. So one of the things that I began to speak aloud was "I get speaking engagements every day—by mail, by phone, and in person." When I began saying this, I hadn't had a single speaking engagement and had never received an invitation to speak anywhere. Eventually, though, I began to receive dozens of invitations every month. God also began opening doors for me to teach His Word on the radio and television, and we began traveling internationally, holding conferences and seminars and doing speaking engagements. The bottom line is, once I got my heart and my mouth in agreement with God's will, God began to move mightily.

Along with thinking about God's promises in His Word and declaring them over my life, I also had to make a daily decision to have an attitude of hope and faith in Him—a positive, confident expectation that God would do something good in my life. God honored my faith and helped me to begin developing a positive, hopeful perspective. I could do that because I had faith that God wanted good for me, not evil (Jer. 29:11; John 10:10). The more I received God's Word, believed it, and spoke His truth when the enemy tempted me to fear, the less Satan was able to manipulate and control me. It didn't take long for me to begin to see radical changes in virtually every area of my life.

I encourage you to open your heart to God and ask Him to show you any area of your life where you are fearful. In those situations, you do not have to allow fear to control you; you can live by faith instead—trusting and resting in God instead of being upset. Fear will attack, but when you stand against it and confront it with the truth of God's Word, fear will lose its hold over your life. The next time fear comes against you, don't say, "I'm afraid…I'm afraid… I'm afraid…" Instead, stir up the faith in your heart and then open your mouth and say, "Something good is going to happen to me! God has a good plan for my life. Through Christ I am more than a conqueror!" (Lam. 3:25; Jer. 29:11;

> *Fear will attack, but when you stand against it and confront it with the truth of God's Word, fear will lose its hold over your life.*

Rom. 8:37). When you resist fear and choose to stand in faith, you shut the door on the enemy and open the door for God's blessings to flow in your life.

Habit Builders

"Have faith in God," Jesus answered. "Truly I tell you, if anyone says to this mountain, 'Go, throw yourself into the sea,' and does not doubt in their heart but believes that what they say will happen, it will be done for them. Therefore I tell you, whatever you ask for in prayer, believe that you have received it, and it will be yours."

Mark 11:22–24

For we live by faith, not by sight.

2 Corinthians 5:7

Now faith is confidence in what
we hope for and assurance
about what we do not see.

Hebrews 11:1

CHAPTER 6
The Habit of Gratitude

We would worry less if we praised more. Thanksgiving is the enemy of discontent and dissatisfaction.

—Harry Ironside

If you are familiar with the miraculous things God did during Old Testament times, you probably remember that God provided the Israelites in the desert with just enough manna for one day's worth of meals (Ex. 16:4). This story provides us with an excellent example of God's will for us. He wants us to live in the present moment. If our minds are focused on what we hope for in the future or what we wish were different about the past, we're not enjoying today. We need to focus on what we're doing now, enjoy every aspect of each day, and be grateful for all the blessings in our lives.

Being thankful for what we already have is an important habit for a godly woman to develop in order to live in peace and joy. Philippians 4:6 says, "Be anxious for nothing, but in everything by prayer and supplication with thanksgiving let your requests be made known to God" (NASB). I remember a time when I asked God to give me something I desired. He showed me that until I stopped complaining about what I already had, there was no point in Him giving me anything else, because I would eventually complain about that, too.

Frankly, I was a little shocked when that happened. But the more I thought about it, the more I realized I had heard the Lord correctly. At the time, I had many things I had once dreamed of and asked God for. If I couldn't be thankful for those blessings, I would ultimately become dissatisfied with the next gift He gave me. This was a powerful lesson in gratitude for me. It also helped me learn not to complain and to realize that no matter what we still desire, we should be grateful for what we already have. When God sees a truly grateful heart, He delights in pouring out blessings and abundance.

Right now, there may be some things in your life that God has graciously provided in response to prayers you have prayed in the past. Perhaps you were thankful for them in the beginning, but now you're dissatisfied again. That's the way human nature is, always wanting more and more. But as we learn to overcome the flesh (our carnal or human nature without

> *When God sees a truly grateful heart, He delights in pouring out blessings and abundance.*

God) and live by the Spirit, we find ourselves empowered to be thankful for what God has given us.

Let us always be grateful for what we have and believe that when we're ready, God will trust us with more.

God wants to give us many good things, but His primary goal is for us to mature spiritually. Third John 2 teaches us that God wants us to prosper and be in good health, even as our souls prosper. A prosperous soul is one that is always growing in godly behavior, which includes gratitude.

Many women are just waiting for something they think of as "good" to happen to them—perhaps falling in love, having a child, succeeding at work, or making some kind of valuable contribution to society. "When that happens," they tell themselves, "I will finally be happy. I'm going to be so thankful!"

Psalm 144:15 says, "Happy and blessed are

the people…whose God is the Lord!" (AMPC). It doesn't say, "Happy is the woman whose circumstances are exactly the way she wants them," or "Happy is the wealthy woman," or "Happy is the famous woman," or "Happy is the woman who has her dream job." No matter what your circumstances may be, you can make a decision to be happy and content *right now*. It honors God greatly when we live with an attitude of gratitude.

According to 1 Thessalonians 5:18, we are to "give thanks in all circumstances." We need to express our gratitude to God and to the people He uses to help and bless us, and we should be thankful for small things as well as big things. We should develop the habit of verbalizing our thanks every chance we get, whether that means saying thank you to a clerk who helps us at a store, a family member who pitches in at home, a colleague who does something nice for us, or a spouse who simply shares life with us faithfully each day. Expressing our gratitude encourages the people we thank. In addition, voicing our thanks is good for us because when we do it, we also remind ourselves afresh of how blessed we are. We can easily start to focus on what we do not have and complain about it, but God looks for people who are thankful and give thanks in all situations.

> *We should develop the habit of verbalizing our thanks every chance we get.*

I encourage you to take some time every day to remember all the things and people God has blessed you with and to speak aloud your thankfulness to them and to the Lord. The more thanks you express, the more grateful you become.

Habit Builders

Give thanks to the LORD,
   for he is good;
his love endures forever.

1 Chronicles 16:34

I will give thanks to you, LORD,
   with all my heart;
I will tell of all your
   wonderful deeds.

Psalm 9:1

And whatever you do, whether in
word or deed, do it all in the name
of the Lord Jesus, giving thanks
to God the Father through him.

Colossians 3:17

CHAPTER 7
The Habit of Trusting God

Trust in the LORD with all your heart and lean not on your own understanding.

—Proverbs 3:5

A woman who develops the habit of trusting God is able to go through life with amazing peace, joy, and confidence. I have learned this through experience and am still growing in this understanding. Trusting God is a process. It's something we grow into, and our trust increases as we continue to experience His goodness and His faithfulness.

Some women were raised in an atmosphere that encourages faith and trust in God, while others, like me, were not. Many of us grew up thinking we had to manage everything ourselves. In the early years of my walk with God, I had to learn to trust Him when I had a problem that seemed too big or too complicated for me to solve. That was a big step for me. Just letting go of a difficult situation and asking God to take care of it for me was a real challenge for me. But over time, I learned to let go, and I began to see that He truly can be trusted.

After a while, I saw that waiting for an emergency or a serious problem before I trusted God was a foolish way to live. I began to realize I did not have the ability to do anything without Him (John 15:5). God led me to realize that we are all truly powerless in our own strength. We need God in *every* situation,

> *Trusting God is a process. It's something we grow into, and our trust increases as we continue to experience His goodness and His faithfulness.*

and we can learn to live every moment in an attitude of trust in Him. Once I recognized my need for God in all things at all times, I began to focus on learning to trust Him in every situation, not just when facing big problems. This relationship of trust comes alive through living with the attitude that God is my helper and my guide and by intentionally choosing to trust Him every day with everything. I have actually formed the habit of confessing my trust and saying, "I trust You, Lord, in all things." I trust Him for specific things I am aware of and for things taking place in my life and in the lives of those I love. But I also trust Him for the things I do not yet know about. "All things" means all things, both seen and unseen, both now and in the future.

One of the Bible verses that taught me to trust God in all things is Psalm 62:8: "Trust in him *at all times,* you people; pour out your hearts to him, for God is our refuge" (emphasis mine). "At all times" and "in all things" convey the same meaning. Neither phrase leaves anything out.

Trusting God is what brings peace into our lives. If we trust Him at all times, in all things, it means we trust Him as much when we do not understand what is going on as we do when we can clearly see what is happening. We trust Him with what we know and with what we don't know. We trust Him just as much when things seem fair or beneficial for us as we do when situations seem unfair or unfavorable for us. We trust Him when everything is going well for us and when nothing seems to be going right.

Trusting God involves some things we may find difficult to do. For example, it requires us to stop trying to manage

> *If we trust God at all times, in all things, it means we trust Him as much when we do not understand what is going on as we do when we can clearly see what is happening.*

or intervene in situations using our natural reasoning, abilities, or strength. We need to have a hands-off policy that gives God room to work. Sometimes it's easy for us to try to solve problems and get involved in situations we think need fixing. We naturally find ourselves being helpers to people around us, and our desires and God-given abilities to help sometimes make us think we need to comment, offer advice, or otherwise be involved in situations when the best approach would be for us to back off, pray, and trust God to work things out.

Trusting God requires patience, and being patient is something many of us are not good at. When we see that something needs to happen, we want it to happen now. When we trust God at all times, that means we also trust Him to bring forth the answer, solution, or breakthrough that is needed at just the right time.

The desire for fast answers and instant

gratification is rampant in our society today. We have lost sight of the fact that waiting can be good for us. Waiting can help us develop the patience we need, and it provides an atmosphere in which faith and trust can deepen. When we seek instant gratification and fail to wait, we can actually thwart God's best intention for us. When we try to impose a human solution in a situation, we miss God's solution—and His way is always best.

I encourage you to develop a habit of trusting God. If you have never been a person who has trusted Him, perhaps you can start the way I did. When you have a problem, choose to release it to Him. Ask Him to take care of it for you, then choose to leave it in His hands and be patient as He works it out. Learn to say, "I trust You, Lord" several times a day. As you continue to walk with God, ask Him to help you grow and reach the point of trusting Him at all times, in all things. If you have already developed the habit of trusting God, there is always room for greater trust and deeper faith. Keep up your good habit of trust, and ask God to strengthen you in it. Although I have learned a great deal about trusting God, there are still times I am tempted to try to handle a situation myself instead of letting Him have it completely. Of course, my efforts do not work, and once again I realize that I need to let go— that God can take care of the situation better than I can.

Habit Builders

The LORD is my strength and my shield;
my heart trusts in him, and he helps me.
My heart leaps for joy, and with
my song I praise him.

Psalm 28:7

Trust in the LORD forever, for the LORD,
the LORD himself, is the Rock eternal.

Isaiah 26:4

And we know that in all things
God works for the good of those
who love him, who have been called
according to his purpose.

Romans 8:28

CHAPTER 8

The Habit of Joy

Happiness depends on happenings; joy depends on Christ.

—Anonymous

Maybe you know someone you would describe as joyful. She almost always has a big smile on her face, she laughs easily and makes others want to laugh too, and she has an optimistic outlook on life, no matter what she faces. She is a delight to have as a friend, she lifts the mood of any group she's in, and others may describe her as "a ray of sunshine." Another way to think of her is as a person full of joy.

While I understand that different people have different personality types and that some are naturally more spunky and outgoing than others, I also believe that each of us can choose to be joyful. We may not have the quickest sense of humor or the ability to light up a room just by walking into it, but that's not what I'm talking about. I'm talking about the joy that comes from knowing God. It is not based on our circumstances but on what we believe.

Joy is a wonderful habit to develop and has many benefits. I think the habit of joy begins with a positive mindset and outlook on life. Anyone who makes a habit of being joyful won't have time for the habit of sadness or the habit of anger. Being joyful makes any situation better and easier to bear, especially difficult ones. Living with joy also makes us strong. Nehemiah 8:10 says that the joy of the Lord is our strength. His joy empowers us to handle any situation

> *Being joyful makes any situation better and easier to bear, especially difficult ones.*

with greater strength than we would have without it.

I've found that the first step to developing a habit of joy is to focus on the positive aspects of your life. No one's life is perfect. There are seasons when many situations are going well and seasons when almost everything seems to be difficult. But no season is 100 percent wonderful or 100 percent terrible. Generally speaking, at any given time in your life, there will be some good things and some difficult things.

I believe we always have more good things in our lives than bad ones, but we need to be mindful to focus on them. Whatever we focus on is what becomes the larger thing to us. For example, if we focus on the hope we have in Christ, we can always expect something good to happen at any moment. That kind of positive expectation releases joy.

Sadly, some people choose to focus on the negative, no matter what else is happening.

They may have just gotten a nice raise, their kids may be doing great socially and in school, they've just lost the twenty pounds they needed to lose, and everyone in the family is healthy. But they aren't happy because they want a bigger house and they don't like their coworkers. Before long, they forget about all the positives in their life and become fixated on what they think they lack. When we choose to focus on the negative, it always leads to sadness, frustration, disappointment, jealousy, or anger.

Choosing to focus on the good things in your life, however, leads to happiness, peace, enthusiasm, and gratitude. It makes us feel good, hopeful, and energized. I have observed that the more people choose to be joyful, the more joy comes their way.

One of the best ways to live a joyful life is to *decide* to be joyful at all times, regardless of your circumstances. Some people say they will rejoice when certain things happen. As I mentioned in the chapter on gratitude, some young women believe their joy will come when certain things happen—when they finish high school, finish college, receive an advanced degree, and land their dream job. Others think they will find joy when they fall in love, get married, buy a house, or have a baby. Women who have had experience with these things often think they will be happy when those babies they wanted so desperately finally move out of the house or give them grandchildren. No matter what a person's journey through life may be, everyone can be tempted to think their joy awaits somewhere in the future when some specific event takes place.

I am a big believer in pursuing dreams and goals, but I also believe that waiting until something desirable happens before you are happy and joyful is a sad way to live. Why? Because the joy that comes with finally reaching a goal or seeing a dream come true doesn't last. It's temporary, and before long, there will be a new vision or desire—and you will tell yourself, "When *that* happens, I will really be happy!" When the fulfillment comes, you'll find that it may have many wonderful qualities, but it will also have some challenges. It may make you happy for a while—just long enough to set a new goal or figure out what you want next. If we walk in the flesh, we are dependent on *things* to make us happy. But if we walk in the Spirit, we are joyful in Christ and in all He has done and is doing in our lives right now.

The way to lasting joy is to choose to be joyful right now. Wherever you are, whatever you're doing, you can decide to focus on everything that is good about it and to rejoice. If you'll do that in every situation, you'll find yourself developing the habit of joy.

I do understand that some situations are very

> *The way to lasting joy is to choose to be joyful right now.*

serious, and some are even tragic. During those times, it would not be appropriate to be laughing or looking for ways to make others laugh. But laughter is not the only way to express joy. You can also be joyful by finding something to be thankful for during difficult times, such as the fact that God loves you and will never leave you. I learned years ago that joy can produce a whole range of emotions, from extreme hilarity to calm delight. In some settings, extreme hilarity would be insensitive, but a quiet, calm delight that keeps your soul at peace would give you strength and hopefully strengthen the people around you.

However you choose to express joy, my point is this: You can be joyful on purpose, and you can incorporate into your life a habit of joy. The more established you become in the habit of joy, the more you will refuse to settle for anything less. Don't put off the joy God has for you. Choose to be joyful today!

Habit Builders

This is the day which the LORD has made;
let us rejoice and be glad in it.

Psalm 118:24 NASB

Shout aloud and sing for joy,
people of Zion, for great is
the Holy One of Israel among you.

Isaiah 12:6

Though you have not seen him,
you love him; and even though you
do not see him now, you believe in him
and are filled with an inexpressible
and glorious joy, for you are
receiving the end result of your faith,
the salvation of your souls.

1 Peter 1:8–9

CHAPTER 9
The Habit of Peace

The world doesn't give peace, for it doesn't have any peace to give. It fights for peace, it negotiates for peace, it maneuvers for peace, but there is no ultimate peace in the world. But Jesus gives peace to those who put their trust in Him.

—Billy Graham

I have heard many women over the years say, "I just want a little peace and quiet." Whether they are running a household with energetic children while trying to hold down a job, raising rebellious teenagers, or juggling their efforts to care for elderly family members while also managing their own lives, there are plenty of opportunities to feel stressed and to cry out for peace. There are also plenty of women who are frightened or concerned about the future, nervous about a medical situation, or anxious about getting their daily needs met, and they crave peace, too.

The enemy will use any type of circumstance to steal our peace. Whatever your situation, I want you to know today that God wants you to make a habit of living at peace. Peace is a fruit of the Holy Spirit (Gal. 5:22), and as a believer in Christ, it is part of your inheritance. This does not mean that you automatically experience and exhibit peace in your life. I wish it were that easy, but peace is something we have to pursue on purpose.

Jesus had a special kind of peace. The apostle Paul refers to this as peace "which transcends all understanding" and says that it will guard our hearts and minds in Christ (Phil. 4:7). Before Jesus ascended to heaven, after He had completed His work on earth, He promised to give His peace to us: "Peace I leave with you; my peace I give you" (John 14:27). The idea in this verse is that Jesus bequeathed His peace to us. *Bequeath* is a term that is used in the execution of a will. When people die, they often bequeath, or will, their finances and possessions—especially things of value—to their loved ones.

When Jesus left this world to go to His Father in heaven, He wanted to make sure that we, His children, inherited the important and valuable gifts we would need to live in power and victory. Included in those gifts was His peace. I believe that Jesus considered peace to be one of the most precious and beneficial gifts He could give to us.

John 14:27 continues: "Do not let your hearts be troubled and do not be afraid." Jesus is basically saying in this verse, "I'm leaving My peace with you, but that doesn't mean that it will just automatically operate. It means that I'm giving you something, a reserve that you can draw on, but you will need to choose to be peaceful on purpose."

It's important to understand that the devil will try any way he can to push you over the edge so you will lose your peace. As I often say, "He sets you up to be upset." Why? Because he knows that if you don't remain peaceful, you can't hear from God, you can't pray, and you can't think clearly.

When people lose their peace and get emotional, they start doing and thinking all kinds of things that don't make sense. They may say things they don't mean. They may buy items they don't really need and can't afford. They may eat when they aren't really hungry. People will do all kinds of things they would not otherwise do when they are upset because they have allowed the devil to steal their peace. But it doesn't have to be that way.

God's peace is ours—the Bible says so. I mentioned earlier that peace is a fruit of the Holy Spirit, who lives inside of all believers. This means that you, as a Christian, have the

> *The devil will try any way he can to push you over the edge so you will lose your peace.*

power to refuse to let negative emotions rule you. You can choose not to allow others to make you unhappy and steal your peace. When you start to get upset about something, make up your mind to stop it immediately and decide, "I am not going to let this upset me. I may not like the situation, but with God's help I will remain at peace in the midst of it."

A helpful Scripture to remember when upsetting circumstances arise is Colossians 3:15:

And let the peace (soul harmony which comes) from Christ rule (act as umpire continually) in your hearts [deciding and settling with finality all questions that arise in your minds, in that peaceful state] to which as [members of Christ's] one body you were also called [to live]. And be thankful (appreciative), [giving praise to God always]. (AMPC)

This verse teaches us to let peace be the "umpire" in our lives, settling every issue that needs a decision. In other words, we decide what stays in our lives and what has to go based on whether or not it brings us peace. To gain and maintain peace in our hearts, we must make decisions based on what God's Word says, not on what we think, what other people tell us to do, or what we hear and see in the media or on the Internet.

Many people go through life making decisions on their own, without consulting the most reliable resource book ever written—the Bible—and too often their decisions bring heartache and trouble. But we can avoid negative outcomes if we seek direction and guidance in God's Word and allow the peace of Christ to rule in our hearts.

No matter what is going on in your life, and especially when you feel upset, you can look to God's Word, find something to settle you down, and allow the presence of peace to help you make decisions and settle with

> *To gain and maintain peace in our hearts, we must make decisions based on what God's Word says.*

finality the questions that are on your mind. Allowing the Word to dwell in your heart and mind will give you the insight, knowledge, and wisdom you need (Col. 3:16). You won't have to be upset about anything, wondering,

"Which direction should I go?" The Word will be a lamp to your feet and a light to your path (Ps. 119:105), and choosing to honor and obey it will bring you peace.

I encourage you to pursue peace and be willing to make whatever adjustments are necessary in your life to become a woman of peace. Being peaceful on purpose is an important secret to living the wonderful life God has planned for you.

Habit Builders

The LORD bless you and keep you;
the LORD make his face shine on you
and be gracious to you;
the LORD turn his face toward you
and give you peace.

Numbers 6:24–26

You will keep in perfect peace those
whose minds are steadfast,
because they trust in you.

Isaiah 26:3

I have told you these things, so that
in me you may have peace.
In this world you will have trouble.
But take heart!
I have overcome the world.

John 16:33

CHAPTER 10

The Habit of Hope

*Yet this I call to mind and therefore I have hope: Because of the L*ORD*'s great love we are not consumed, for his compassions never fail.*
—Lamentations 3:21–22

Hope is one of my favorite habits, and I'd like to share with you part of my story about becoming a hopeful person, one who wakes up every day expecting good things to happen to me. Many years ago I had an extremely negative attitude about my life because of the devastating abuse that had taken place in my past. That abuse had many negative effects, and one of them was that I *expected* people to hurt me—and they did. I *expected* people to be dishonest with me—and they were. I was afraid to believe that anything good might happen in my life. I had wanted positive things to happen in the past and had been disappointed repeatedly, so I finally reached the point where I gave up hope. I truly thought I was protecting myself from being hurt by not expecting anything good to happen. My attitude was: "If you don't expect anything good to happen, then you won't be disappointed when it doesn't."

When I really began to study the Bible and trust God to heal and restore me, I began to realize that my negative attitudes had to go. I needed to let go of my past and move into the future with hope, faith, and trust in God. I needed healing from the heaviness of despair, depression, and discouragement I had carried for so long. And, with God's help, I worked through various issues and began to experience the healing I needed. Once I dug into the truth of what the Bible says about me and about my attitudes toward life, I began to turn my negative thoughts and words into positive ones (you can read about that in chapter 11). The blessings and good changes that began to happen in my life as a result of simply becoming hopeful and optimistic were amazing!

Now, I'm not saying that we can get whatever we want just by thinking about it. God has a perfect plan for each of us, and we can't control Him with our thoughts and words—but we can think and speak truths that are based on His Word and that agree with His will and plan for our lives.

We can practice being positive in every situation that arises. Even if what is taking place in our lives at the moment seems negative, we can choose to expect God to bring good out of it, just as He has promised in His Word

(Rom. 8:28). We must understand that before our lives can change, our attitudes must change.

Without hope, people become depressed, discouraged, despondent, and filled with fear. But Psalm 42:5 encourages us to "hope in God *and* wait expectantly for Him" (AMP). God wants to be good to you. Lamentations 3:25 assures us that "the LORD is good to those whose hope is in him, to the one who seeks him."

> *Even if what is taking place in our lives at the moment seems negative, we can choose to expect God to bring good out of it, just as He has promised in His Word.*

Hope is a powerful spiritual force, but it is only activated through our faith and positive attitudes. And our attitudes have to be based on more than how we feel or what we see around us. They must be grounded in what we *know* from God's Word to be true and in our belief that God is good.

Most of us struggle to believe that God is working to bless us or help us until we see something happening with our natural eyes, but this usually isn't the way God works. He works behind the scenes much of the time. He often spends years preparing us for something good that will manifest in our lives in seemingly sudden ways. The fact that we cannot see what God is doing does not mean He is idle on our behalf. Right now, even as you are reading this book, God is working on your behalf and moving forward His good plan for your life—a plan for positive things, not negative, hurtful things.

I urge you to allow hope and faith to operate in your life right now. Without them, life isn't enjoyable. Every time I fail to apply faith and hope in my life, I stop believing, and I lose my peace. And as soon as I lose my peace, my joy goes with it. No matter what your life has been like until now, it's vital for you to believe that it can change. Faith and hope are the keys to a brighter, more positive future.

Jeremiah 29:11 is a great Scripture to memorize if you want to develop the habit of hope: "'For I know the plans I have for you,' declares the LORD, 'plans to prosper you and not to harm you, plans to give you hope and a future.'" You can be assured that God has a good plan for your life, so start trusting Him today. Believing God for good things brings you peace and rest and puts an end to discouragement and anxiety while you're waiting for them to manifest.

> *No matter what your life has been like until now, it's vital for you to believe that it can change. Faith and hope are the keys to a brighter, more positive future.*

No matter how hopeless your situation seems to be or how long it has been that way, I know that it can change. No matter how tempted you are to give up hope, I know you can change, because

I did. It took time and a strong commitment to maintaining a healthy, positive attitude, but it was worth it. And it will be worth it for you, too. Whatever happens, develop a strong habit of hope in the Lord. He wants to be good to you, and I urge you to believe that something good is going to happen in your life at any moment!

Habit Builders

Why, my soul, are you downcast?
Why so disturbed within me?
Put your hope in God, for I will yet
praise him, my Savior and my God.

Psalm 42:11

But those who hope in the LORD will
renew their strength. They will soar
on wings like eagles; they will run

and not grow weary, they will walk
and not be faint.

Isaiah 40:31

May the God of hope fill you with
all joy and peace as you trust in him,
so that you may overflow with hope
by the power of the Holy Spirit.

Romans 15:13

CHAPTER 11

The Habit of Positive Thoughts and Words

The positive thinker sees the invisible, feels the intangible, and achieves the impossible.
—Winston Churchill

If you are familiar with my teachings, you know that I write and speak often about the power of thoughts and words. I cannot overemphasize how powerful our thinking and our words are; they have tremendous impact on every aspect of our lives. We can literally change our lives by changing our thoughts and our words. I have seen this in my own life and in the lives of more people around me than I can count. Now, of course, if we want change, we want it to be good, not bad. So when we consider our habits regarding thoughts and words, we're looking to make them more positive, not more negative. Positive thoughts and words, with God's help, will transform us into positive people.

The first step toward becoming a positive person is to think positive thoughts. In fact, it would be impossible to become a positive person without developing a positive mindset. Philippians 4:8 teaches us to think about things that are "excellent" and "praiseworthy," which is a way of encouraging us to train our minds to think optimistically. It offers us specific examples of things to think about, such as things that are true, noble, right, pure, lovely, and admirable. If we were to refuse to think thoughts that don't fall into one of the categories on this list, we would go a long way toward developing the habit of thinking positively. According to Proverbs 23:7, we become what we think. In other words, our thoughts shape our lives, and that is one reason I have spent years emphasizing them in my ministry.

The apostle Paul writes in 2 Corinthians 10:5 that as Christians, we are to "take captive every thought to make it obedient to Christ." Think about that: When people are taken captive, they cannot do whatever they want to do; they are not free. That's the way we are to handle our thoughts. We shouldn't let them be free to roam around in our minds, causing us to think whatever comes along.

Let me ask you: Do you take captive the negative thoughts that enter your mind, begging for you to dwell on them? When you recognize that a thought is not good, do you take action to get it out of your mind, or are you passive about it, choosing to let it settle into your thinking and influence your mood?

Sometimes people rationalize the failure to be diligent about their thoughts by telling themselves, *These are just thoughts. No one can see them or hear them. No one knows about them except me.* The fact that thoughts are invisible and inaudible is not the point. The point is that although you may think they are limited to your own mind, God knows them, and they are very powerful. They have a major impact on you, whether anyone else knows them or not. Negative thoughts can poison our words, our behavior, and our lives. They precede our words and actions; therefore, we must deal with them first. Our thoughts about other people will determine how we treat them. It is not possible to be loving toward someone if our thoughts about them are unloving.

This may be a new idea to you, but it's true: You can think whatever you choose to think.

You don't have to accept whatever pops into your mind. You can evaluate it and choose whether to keep it in your thought process or not. You can decide to switch from a negative thought to a positive one almost immediately, and I hope you will begin right away to develop that habit or strengthen it if you are already doing it, because it will bring much joy and peace to your life. Apart from Jesus we can do nothing (John 15:5), so always remember to ask for His help.

Speaking positive words is as important as thinking positive thoughts. Proverbs 8:6 says, "Listen, for I have trustworthy things to say; I open my lips to speak what is right." I like this verse, and it is a great example for us to follow because it shows us the writer's decision about how to speak. Just as we can choose

> *This may be a new idea to you, but it's true: You can think whatever you choose to think.*

our thoughts, we can direct our words with God's help. Proverbs 18:21 teaches us that "the tongue has the power of life and death." Our words affect us and the people around us. They also affect our walk with God. As I have said many times, we cannot have a negative mouth and a positive life.

One way to view the principle set forth in Proverbs 18:21 is to say that our words are containers for power. They are a force—either positive or negative—for those who speak them and for the people who hear them. Because of this, we should not just say whatever comes to mind, but we should choose our words carefully. Our words can

> *Our words affect us and the people around us. They also affect our walk with God.*

encourage or discourage; they can be constructive or destructive; they can help people feel better or make them feel worse. The tongue is a very small part of the body, but it can have a tremendous impact (James 3:3–6).

Understanding the power of words is both a privilege and a responsibility. It is a privilege because if we choose our words well, we can benefit others and reap blessings for ourselves. It is a responsibility because we need to take seriously the fact that we can decide how we want to use the influence of our words, and God's Word holds us accountable to use them in positive ways. I spent almost forty years of my life not understanding the difference my thoughts and words made in the quality of my life. I am grateful to know it now and to have had time to develop the habit of positive thoughts and words. I challenge you to build that habit, too, and I can assure you that you'll be glad you did.

Habit Builders

The soothing tongue is a tree of life,
but a perverse tongue crushes the spirit.

Proverbs 15:4

What goes into someone's mouth
does not defile them, but what
comes out of their mouth,
that is what defiles them.

Matthew 15:11

Set your minds on things above,
not on earthly things.

Colossians 3:2

CHAPTER 12

The Habit of Receiving God's Forgiveness

God takes our sins—the past, present, and future, and dumps them in the sea and puts up a sign that says, NO FISHING ALLOWED.
—Corrie ten Boom

Forgiveness is among many important habits for a godly woman to develop. The word *forgiveness* can refer to the forgiveness that God extends to us through His Son, Jesus, or to the forgiveness we extend to people who hurt or offend us. There is also forgiveness we grant ourselves when we have failed or made mistakes.

In this chapter, I want to write about the forgiveness God offers us, and in the next chapter I will focus on the importance of forgiving others. Nobody goes through this life without sinning and needing God to forgive them. If we don't learn to receive God's forgiveness, we will stay stuck in feelings of guilt and regret, never moving beyond them into the good things He has in store for us.

The first step toward receiving God's forgiveness is to recognize and acknowledge our sin and to repent. This takes humility, which is fairly easy for some women but more difficult for those who may have spent years rationalizing sinful attitudes and behaviors of blaming others for the problems sin has produced in their lives. According to Romans 3:23, no one is exempt from sinning; everyone does it: "All have sinned and fall short of the glory of God."

Sin separates us from God. The fact that we sin does not mean we are not saved; it simply means that the intimate fellowship we can enjoy with God is broken. It hinders our prayers and may cause us to be unable to hear God's voice. When we sin, God does not turn His back on us; He looks on us with compassion because of His love for us, convicts us (not condemns us) by the Holy Spirit, and lets us know that we can be forgiven and restored.

If we don't learn to receive God's forgiveness, we will stay stuck in feelings of guilt and regret, never moving beyond them into the good things He has in store for us.

There was a time in my life when I didn't understand the difference between conviction and condemnation, and I think many other people may not understand it. I have learned that conviction is from the Holy Spirit and is intended to help me recognize my sin, repent, and overcome it with His help. It is the gentle whisper of the Holy Spirit letting me know my behavior doesn't please the Lord. It is a sign of God's love, for He only chastises (corrects and disciplines) those He loves (Rev. 3:19; Heb. 12:6).

Condemnation is from the devil, and it causes us to feel guilty and discouraged, but it does nothing to help us. The more we love God, the more our sin bothers us. As we grow in love for Him, we grow in our hatred for sin because we know that God hates sin. I am grateful each time the Holy Spirit convicts me of sin because it helps me recognize areas in my life that need to change.

Once we acknowledge our sin and repent, we can be assured that God has forgiven us. One of my favorite Scripture passages on this topic is 1 John 1:8–9: "If we say that we have no sin, we are deceiving ourselves and the truth is not in us. If we confess our sins,

He is faithful and righteous to forgive us our sins and to cleanse us from *all* unrighteousness" (NASB, italics mine).

This verse in the Amplified Bible, Classic Edition says that God "continuously" cleanses us from all sin. I believe this teaches us that as long as we stay in fellowship with God, being quick to confess and repent of our sins, He is always cleansing us. Note also that He cleanses us from "all unrighteousness." He doesn't forgive some sins and not others, or forgive some a lot and others just a little. His forgiveness is thorough, and it covers each and every sin we commit. Nothing you or I can do is beyond God's compassion, love, and forgiveness.

Just as we have all sinned and fallen short of God's glory, we are also all justified and put into right relationship with God through the redemption Jesus Christ provided for us at the cross (Rom. 3:23–24). To be justified by God means that all of our sins are pardoned and that in His sight we are made just as though we have never sinned. Once we receive God's forgiveness, we are clean. When He washes us from our sin, He holds nothing against us. Because this is true, we have no reason to wallow in guilt, condemnation, or anger toward ourselves. We honor God by accepting His forgiveness, not by continuing to make efforts to pay for our sin or punish ourselves for it.

> *Once we receive God's forgiveness, we are clean.*

God has His own way of dealing with our sin, and that is to forgive it. We can't do anything to earn His forgiveness or to compensate for our sin, and if we try, we insult what He has done for us. God's forgiveness is a gift, and the proper response is for us to receive and be thankful for such a blessing.

It's important to understand that there is a difference between asking for God's forgiveness and receiving it. His forgiveness is a finished work. It's always available to you. All you have to do is repent and ask for it. But after you ask God to forgive you for something, take a moment to sit in His presence and meditate on what forgiveness really means and how much God loves you. Tell Him that you receive the forgiveness He has given you and that you are grateful for it. And when you are tempted to return to your guilt and shame about the sin for which you have received forgiveness, remember that God has taken your guilt away and that you can let it go—forever—just as God has.

Part of repentance is learning not to repeat the same things over and over and falling into habitual sin. The Holy Spirit empowers us to stand aggressively against temptation and to say no to sin. When you have been forgiven for something, it's a good idea to also ask God to give you strength to turn away from that thought, attitude, or behavior so you won't do it again. This doesn't mean you will never struggle with the same sin in the future, but God's forgiveness is always available to you. As you continue to fellowship with Jesus and grow in your relationship with Him, you will sin less and less, and sin will have less and less power over your life.

There is no limit to how many times God will forgive us, but He also wants us to grow stronger in our ability to resist sin. God changes us little by little (2 Cor. 3:18), and part of that process of maturity involves confessing our sin, repenting, receiving His forgiveness, and growing in obedience to Him as He leads us to become all He wants us to be.

Habit Builders

Then I acknowledged my sin to you
and did not cover up my iniquity.
I said, "I will confess my transgressions
to the LORD." And you
forgave the guilt of my sin.

Psalm 32:5

You, Lord, are forgiving and good,
abounding in love to all who call to you.

Psalm 86:5

In him we have redemption through
his blood, the forgiveness of sins,
in accordance with the riches
of God's grace.

Ephesians 1:7

CHAPTER 13

The Habit of Extending Forgiveness to Others

Forgive, forget. Bear with the faults of others as you would have them bear with yours. Be patient and understanding. Life is too short to be vengeful or malicious.

—Phillips Brooks

Being human and being alive means that at some point in our journey through life, we will be wounded or disappointed by other people. If we don't develop the habit of learning to forgive others, we will be trapped in anger and bitterness, unable to find peace or to develop and maintain the kinds of healthy relationships God wants us to enjoy.

Jesus died for us so that our sins might be forgiven, allowing us to be restored to an intimate relationship with God through Him. His gift of forgiveness is so awesome that it's almost unfathomable in its perfection, and it's a gift that we need on a regular basis. What God has given us freely—forgiveness of sin—He expects us to give freely to others (Matt. 10:8). Because we can count on being forgiven when we repent of our sin, we can also live with the willingness to forgive others when they hurt or offend us.

> *Because we can count on being forgiven when we repent of our sin, we can also live with the willingness to forgive others when they hurt or offend us.*

Many people view forgiving others as something we are "supposed" to do if we are Christians, and it is certainly part of Christian behavior. People may also think of it as doing something kind for the person who has wounded them, but I've learned to look at it a bit differently. I have come to see extending forgiveness to people as also doing myself a favor. When I forgive, I am no longer burdened with the negative emotions that accompany unforgiveness. It sets me free to pray for them and bless them instead of hating them and wishing them harm. Seeing forgiveness from this perspective makes it much easier for me to quickly and thoroughly forgive others. As a godly woman, getting into the habit of forgiving people promptly and completely will make the rest of your life happier and your relationships healthier.

The most effective way I know to begin to forgive the people who have hurt you is to practice the three D's of forgiveness: desire, decide, and depend. The first step toward forgiveness is to *desire* to do it because of your love for God. The desire is based on your relationship with God and wanting to obey Him, not necessarily because you feel the person who hurt you deserves your forgiveness any more than we deserve God's forgiveness toward us.

When we think about how God forgives us and how He asks us in His Word to forgive others, our love for Him compels us to want to obey. Based on our desire, we then *decide*—make a deliberate choice—to forgive. This kind of decision is not emotional; it is a decision we must make on purpose and with determination to stand firm. When we make the decision, we don't rehearse the wrongs done against us or consult our feelings. We simply choose to forgive because we know that is what God would have us to do. Third, we *depend* on the Holy Spirit to help us carry out our decision. Forgiveness isn't easy, and we need supernatural strength to extend it to others.

After we have desired and decided to forgive, and depended on the Holy Spirit to help us do it, we need to take one more step, which is to pray for those who have hurt us. Jesus says in Matthew 5:43–45:

You have heard that it was said, "Love your neighbor and hate your enemy." But I tell you, love your enemies and pray for those who persecute you, that you may be children of your Father in heaven. He causes his sun to rise on the evil and the good, and sends rain on the righteous and the unrighteous.

I want to mention that this passage of Scripture is not instructing us to let people hurt us or walk all over us while we never confront them about their words or actions. Forgiveness is not about that, but about the attitude of our hearts toward people. It means that we set them free from what they have done to us, but it does not necessarily mean we remain in the same type of relationship we have always had with them. We can forgive people, bless them, and be kind to them while still relating to them in ways that are healthy, not hurtful, for us. We can pray for those who wound us because we understand that hurting people hurt people. We know that they are hurting and that God can heal them and make them whole, just as He can heal us from the wounds their behavior has inflicted on our souls.

I want to reiterate that forgiveness is not an emotional decision, meaning that we don't forgive because we feel like it. We rarely feel like doing it. So once you have been through the process of forgiveness, your emotions and feelings toward the

> *We can forgive people, bless them, and be kind to them while still relating to them in ways that are healthy, not hurtful, for us.*

person you have forgiven, or toward whatever happened that hurt you, may not change for a while. However, your emotions will ultimately catch up with your decision if you stand firm in choosing to forgive and continue praying for the person who hurt you. You will learn to manage your emotions and stay steady, and you can do so with the help of the Holy Spirit.

God wants you to be strong, joyful, peaceful, and free. Holding on to unforgiveness will hinder these good qualities, but forgiving people who have hurt you will release them in your life.

Now, I want to ask you to do something that may seem unusual. I'd like for you to reread this chapter with this in mind: Not only do other people hurt us; sometimes we hurt ourselves. It can be more difficult to forgive ourselves than to forgive anyone else. But we see in this chapter that forgiveness is critical to healthy relationships, and we definitely have a relationship with ourselves. Sometimes the person you need to forgive the most may be yourself, because you must relate well to yourself so you can move forward into all God has for you. Will you do that? And if you need to forgive yourself, I beg you, please do. Forgiving yourself is how you receive God's forgiveness. He is extending a wonderful gift to you, and all you need to do is receive it and be thankful.

Habit Builders

Then Peter came to Jesus and asked, "Lord, how many times shall I forgive my brother or sister who sins against me? Up to seven times?" Jesus answered, "I tell you, not seven times, but seventy-seven times."

Matthew 18:21–22

Do not judge, and you will not be judged.
Do not condemn, and you will
not be condemned.
Forgive, and you will be forgiven.

Luke 6:37

Be kind and compassionate to
one another, forgiving each other,
just as in Christ God forgave you.

Ephesians 4:32

CHAPTER 14

The Habit of Enjoying Each Day

There is nothing dreary and doubtful about [life]. It is meant to be continually joyful… We are called to a settled happiness in the Lord whose joy is our strength.

—Amy Carmichael

For many years, I was a person who did not enjoy life, let alone celebrate it. I worked hard and achieved quite a bit, but I never took the time to enjoy the fruit of my labors. I was a Christian who was on my way to heaven, but

I was not enjoying the trip. Since those days, God has taught me a great deal about how to enjoy life. John 10:10 says that Jesus came that we might "have *and* enjoy life, and have it in abundance (to the full, till it overflows)" (AMPC). The quality of life that Jesus offers us is beyond anything we could ever find on earth or create for ourselves.

One of the most important lessons I have learned about enjoying life is that our ability to enjoy it is not based on having circumstances we consider enjoyable. Enjoying life is an attitude of the heart. For years, I wanted and tried to change people and situations so they would make me happy. Once I discovered that the world was not going to change to accommodate me, I decided to adjust my approach to some of the situations I faced. I also decided to try to find a way to enjoy everything I did, which included my work and tasks that were not pleasant for me. If we cannot enjoy what we are doing, we can at least enjoy Jesus while we do it. These decisions made a remarkable difference in my life, and I believe with all my heart that they will help you, too.

We face many pressures. But as women who walk with God, although we do live in a pressure-filled world, we also have available to us the abundant quality of life that comes from God—a life that is not characterized by fear, stress, worry, or despair. God is not impatient or in a hurry. He takes time to enjoy everything He has made. And He wants us to do the same.

I have met many women who are not enjoying their lives, and that always saddens me. They may be juggling many different things, but they are doing so while feeling stressed and weary. They are

> *One of the most important lessons I have learned about enjoying life is that our ability to enjoy it is not based on having circumstances we consider enjoyable.*

carrying heavy loads, and they are tired. Their high-pressure lifestyles can even cause health problems, which add even more stress.

There's got to be a solution. And there is.

Jesus understands stress and tiredness. In Matthew 11:28–29, He says, "Come to me, all you who are weary and burdened, and I will give you rest. Take my yoke upon you and learn from me, for I am gentle and humble in heart, and you will find rest for your souls."

So how do we come to Jesus so He will give us rest? He tells us how to do it in Matthew 18:3: "Truly I tell you, unless you change and become like little children, you will never enter the kingdom of heaven." What are little children like? They are trusting, loving, and forgiving. They enjoy simplicity—and they find all kinds of things to laugh about and ways to enjoy life. Laughter is a great stress reliever!

God wants us to approach life with child-like faith. He wants us to grow up in our behavior and to be mature but at the same time to remain childlike in our attitude of trust and dependence on Him. He wants us to know that we are His precious children and to rest in His care for us. We demonstrate our faith in Him when we come to Him with these attributes. I do not believe we can have peace and enjoy life without childlike faith. When we begin to live with all the simplicity and innocence of a child, it changes our whole outlook in a most amazing way.

Let me encourage you to start looking for ways that you may be complicating the way you approach your relationship with God. By this, I mean that perhaps you overcomplicate your faith, or you try to reason your way through your relationship with Him, or you don't feel free to relax and experience joy in your spiritual life because you think God may not approve. Or perhaps you aren't willing to ask for God's help when you need it because you think you should be strong enough or smart enough to manage life on your own. Ask the Holy Spirit to teach you how to enjoy your life by teaching you childlike faith. He lives in you (1 Cor. 3:16), and although He is extraordinarily powerful, He is also extraordinarily simple. He likes to make relationship with Him easy for us, not difficult or burdensome. He will teach you how to enjoy your life if you truly wish to learn.

For years, one hindrance to my ability to enjoy life was that I was a workaholic. I found extreme satisfaction in accomplishment, and I often worked when I should have taken the time to do other things—maybe even to spend time having fun with my family. Take it from me: Enjoying life is a gift from God! Our families and friends are also His gift to us. Don't risk having an unbalanced attitude that might lead the people close to you to believe they are less important to you than your busyness and your work. Don't allow yourself to get so caught up in that trap that you fail to enjoy the simple or seemingly small pleasures that God provides each day.

God has given you life, and He wants you to enjoy every bit of it and live it "to the full," as Jesus said in John 10:10. A great way to start every new day is with this confession based on Psalm 118:24: "This is the day which the Lord has made; I will rejoice and be glad in it!" (NASB).

It is God's will that you enjoy your life. That doesn't mean that you spend all of your time entertaining yourself; it means that you learn to enjoy ordinary, daily activities because you are doing them with and for the Lord.

> *Don't risk having an unbalanced attitude that might lead the people close to you to believe they are less important to you than your busyness and your work.*

Habit Builders

You make known to me the path of life;
you will fill me with joy in your
presence, with eternal pleasures
at your right hand.

Psalm 16:11

Rejoice in the Lord always.
I will say it again: Rejoice!

Philippians 4:4

Rejoice always, pray continually,
give thanks in all circumstances;
for this is God's will for you
in Christ Jesus.

1 Thessalonians 5:16–18

CHAPTER 15

The Habit of Decisiveness

In any moment of decision, the best thing you can do is the right thing, the next best thing you can do is the wrong thing, and the worst thing you can do is nothing.

—Theodore Roosevelt

We women have taken some teasing through the years about our supposed inability to make up our minds. And although we're well aware that indecisiveness is not limited to women, I'm sure we are all aware that it is not unusual for us to change our minds about certain things.

I'm sure you know what I'm talking about. It may be as simple as putting on a certain outfit as you're getting ready for the day and then thinking, for no apparent reason, *I don't really want to wear this today. I think I'll wear something else.* You may tell your husband or a friend in the morning that you want an Italian meal for dinner, but by late afternoon you've decided you'd rather have a steak.

There may be moments when you're calm, peaceful, and certain of yourself in a specific situation and moments when you feel anxious, worried, and insecure about the very same thing. You may make a decision about something and be sure about it—and then later realize that you're confused and hesitant about what you were so clear and certain of only a few moments earlier.

There have been many times in my life when I have experienced indecision. Sometimes I seemed to be able to make a decision easily

and stick with it. Then, at other times, I struggled to arrive at a decision at all. Doubt, fear,
and uncertainty haunted me. I went back and
forth between two opinions. I second-guessed
myself and could not make up my mind.

For a long time, I didn't know I could do
anything about my thoughts. I assumed I
was destined to be indecisive. I believed in
God—and had for many years—but I'd had no
exposure at all to biblical teaching about my
thoughts or about the proper condition of a
believer's mind.

As I became much more serious about my
relationship with the Lord and more committed to living by His Word, I learned that many
of my problems with indecision were rooted
in wrong thought patterns and insecurity. My
mind was undisciplined and ever changing.

I felt overwhelmed when I began to see how
indecisive and insecure I was. I tried hard to
correct the problem by rejecting the wrong

thoughts that came into my mind, but they were persistent.

Many women struggle with this same problem because they have spent years allowing their minds to wander. They don't realize they can change the way they think, so they've never applied the principles of discipline to their thought lives. People who cannot seem to concentrate long enough to make a decision often think there is something wrong with their minds. However, the inability to concentrate and settle on a decision can be the result of years of simply letting the mind do whatever it wants to do. Also, it is often tied to a lack of confidence, self-doubt, and insecurity. But I have good news: The more you learn about God's guidance and the wisdom He has placed inside of you, the more you will be able to trust that you can and do make good decisions.

I struggled for years with the lack of ability to make firm decisions that I could stick with.

When circumstances in my life called for an important decision, I found that I wasn't confident or disciplined enough to step out and make it and then hold to it. But I eventually became very decisive, and you can as well.

If you have a hard time concentrating, read these words in Ecclesiastes 5:1, and they will help you: "Give your mind to what you are doing" (AMPC). On my journey toward becoming decisive, I finally realized I had to train my mind through discipline to remain focused on the moment I was in, and so do you. While trying to complete a project, do you ever suddenly realize that your mind has just wandered off onto something that has absolutely nothing to do with the issue at hand? I have, but

The more you learn about God's guidance and the wisdom He has placed inside of you, the more you will be able to trust that you can and do make good decisions.

through God's grace and disciplining my mind, I have improved little by little.

Sometimes my mind even wanders off during conversations. There are times when Dave is talking to me, and I listen for a while— then all of a sudden I realize that I have not heard a word he's been saying. Why? Because I allowed my mind to veer onto something else. My body was standing there, apparently listening, but in my mind, nothing he said registered.

For a long time, when this sort of thing happened, I pretended that I knew exactly what Dave was saying. Now I simply stop and say, "I'm sorry, but can you back up and repeat that? I let my mind wander, and I didn't hear everything you said." In this way, I am dealing with the problem and disciplining my mind to stay on track. Confronting this issue is the only way to overcome it.

The mind is a battlefield. The enemy fights

for your attention and wants you to think the thoughts he wants you to think, not the ones God wants you to think. Indecision and uncertainty are often results of losing these battles, and they can cause you to wonder if there is something wrong with your mind. But the truth is, your thoughts just need to be disciplined. Ask God to help you, and then refuse to allow your mind to think about whatever it pleases. Begin today to control your thoughts, with God's help, and to keep your mind on what you're doing or what others are saying. You'll need to practice for a while, because breaking old habits and forming new ones always takes time. Discipline is not fun when we are applying it, but it's always worth it in the end. When you win the

> *The mind is a battlefield. The enemy fights for your attention and wants you to think the thoughts he wants you to think, not the ones God wants you to think.*

battle for your mind, you'll be much more certain of yourself and develop the habit of being decisive as you become a godly woman who can make up her mind with confidence.

Habit Builders

Whether you turn to the right or
to the left, your ears will hear
a voice behind you, saying,
"This is the way; walk in it."

Isaiah 30:21

Those who live according to the flesh have
their minds set on what the flesh desires;
but those who live in accordance with
the Spirit have their minds set on what the
Spirit desires. The mind governed
by the flesh is death, but the mind
governed by the Spirit is life and peace.

The mind governed by the flesh is hostile
to God; it does not submit to God's law,
nor can it do so.

Romans 8:5–7

But when you ask, you must believe
and not doubt, because the one who
doubts is like a wave of the sea,
blown and tossed by the wind.
That person should not expect to
receive anything from the Lord.
Such a person is double-minded
and unstable in all they do.

James 1:6–8

CHAPTER 16
The Habit of Stability

My heart, O God, is steadfast, my heart is steadfast.

—Psalm 57:7

One of the outstanding habits in the life of a godly woman, I believe, should be emotional stability—the ability to stay emotionally balanced and composed in any given situation, no matter what the circumstances. The Old Testament king Solomon, who wrote most of the book of Proverbs, refers to this in Proverbs 16:32: "Better a patient person than a warrior, one with self-control than one who takes a city." We are women, after all, and we experience a wide range of God-given emotions that can be beneficial when led by the Holy Spirit. But many women allow their feelings to go unrestrained; that kind of emotional roller coaster is a really hard place for any woman to live, and it makes her difficult to live with. In order to get emotional stability, we must make the quality decision that we are not going to live according to our feelings.

Dave has always been very stable emotionally. For example, there have been times I've heard people begin to talk negatively about us and it made me nervous, but Dave would say, "We don't have the problem; those who are talking

> *In order to get emotional stability, we must make the quality decision that we are not going to live according to our feelings.*

about us do. Our hearts are right before God, so why should we be bothered? Let's just relax and trust the Lord to handle everything."

Dave's steadfast, unchanging character reminds me of a rock, which is one of the names given to Jesus (1 Cor. 10:4). Jesus is called the Rock because He is solid and stable, "the same yesterday and today and forever" (Heb. 13:8). Jesus did not allow Himself to be moved or to be led by His emotions even though He was subject to the same feelings that we are. Instead, He chose to be led by the Spirit.

There came a time in my life when I wanted to be more like Dave, who was more like Jesus than I was. Dave says he can remember years ago when he would drive home from work in the evening, thinking, *I wonder what Joyce will be like tonight? Will she be happy or angry, talkative or quiet, in a good mood or a bad mood?* The way he left me in the morning might not be the way he found me in the evening. My soul (my mind, will, and emotions)—rather than my spirit—controlled me, because I had not yet studied God's Word to the point that the Holy Spirit could use it to renew my mind and heal and strengthen my emotions.

For example, I was addicted to excitement. I found it difficult to settle down and live an ordinary, everyday life—relaxing and enjoying my husband, my children, and the home God had given me. I had to have something exciting going on all the time. And I'm not saying it's wrong to be excited at times, but it is danger-ous to need or crave excitement or to be exces-sive about it.

Many women need to be careful about becoming all "hyped up" about things, because often hype leads to disappointment. I'll give you an illustration to make my point. I would get all worked up about going on vacation. If the trip was postponed or didn't turn out the way I expected, I would experience an emotional low.

It would have been better for me (and my entire family) to view things with flexibility and a steady determination to accept whatever happened and enjoy it than to build things up in my mind, expecting them to be a certain way. Jesus said in John 15:11 that He wanted His joy—meaning "calm delight"—to be in us, "complete *and* overflowing" (AMPC).

These days I may still get excited about planning certain things, but I don't feel extreme emotions over them. I maintain a calm delight, and I don't allow my emotions to get revved up and dependent on having my plan turn out perfectly. That way, if things don't turn out the way I thought they would, my emotions won't plummet.

God desires for us to be well balanced. If you have been the type of woman I once was, who was careful not to have any expectations at all so I would never be disappointed, that isn't a balanced position to take, either. It's true that every single day is not going to be gloriously exciting. There will be days when God brings excitement into our lives, but we cannot spend the majority of our lives seeking excitement. There will also be days when the storms of life rage around us, and we may be tempted to feel afraid, anxious, or hopeless. In Psalm 143:10, David said to the Lord, "May your good Spirit lead me on level ground."

I love that prayer of David's. Don't you want your heart and mind to live on level ground? I do. You are probably thinking, *I have this same problem you had, Joyce, but how can I change?* Here is an important key to change and spiritual growth: You have to be willing to let your flesh suffer when you choose what you know is right. You can't deny the existence of your feelings, but you can channel them in the right direction, finding

> *You have to be willing to let your flesh suffer when you choose what you know is right.*

the place of balance that brings peace. Allowing the flesh to suffer while its power over you is weakening is not pleasant, but experiencing the best God has for you is impossible without it (Rom. 8:16–17).

As I grew in my relationship with the Lord and in the knowledge of His Word over the years, I began to be convicted in my heart that I was behaving badly when my emotions were out of balance. I had a choice to make at that point: I could either keep acting in ways I knew were not pleasing to God (and were, in fact, hurting my family), or do what I knew Jesus would do, even though my flesh was screaming and pressuring me to continue letting it be in control. The journey to emotional stability is worth taking.

God does not expect you to be perfect. He just wants you to keep moving toward Him, aligning your will with His, and letting Him develop emotional stability and self-control in you. Having emotions is not a sin—it's what we do with them that matters.

When everything is going as we'd like it to go, we can easily remain stable. But when life's storms arise, our emotions tend to get tossed every which way the wind blows. Submit yourself and any situation that causes your emotions to dictate how you act to God, and choose to refuse to give in to them. Ask God to give you the ability to be calm and steady in every situation, even very difficult ones (Ps. 94:13), and to help you make a habit of living that way. He loves you and desires to bless you with emotional strength and stability.

Habit Builders

A hot-tempered person stirs up conflict, but the one who is patient calms a quarrel.

Proverbs 15:18

Fools give full vent to their rage,
but the wise bring calm in the end.

Proverbs 29:11

My dear brothers and sisters,
take note of this: Everyone should
be quick to listen, slow to speak
and slow to become angry,
because human anger does not produce
the righteousness that God desires.

James 1:19–20

CHAPTER 17

The Habit of Releasing Your Worries

Worry is a cycle of inefficient thoughts whirling around a center of fear.

—Corrie ten Boom

Worry—feeling uneasy, troubled, anxious, and burdened by cares and concerns—seems to plague multitudes of women in our world today. It is human nature to be concerned about the unsettling situations that exist in our world and in our personal lives, but God offers us another way to live. He offers us the opportunity to turn all of our worries and cares over to Him and be at peace while He provides the answers we need.

Worry is the opposite of faith, and it is a detrimental habit. It steals our peace, wears us out physically, and can even make us sick. Worry is caused by not trusting God to take care of the various situations we face. Too often we trust our own abilities, believing we can figure out how to take care of our own problems. Yet sometimes, after all our worry and effort to go it alone, we come up short, unable to bring about suitable solutions.

The Bible has much to say about how we are to handle worry and the emotions that go along with it. When I think about these things, 1 Peter 5:7 always comes to my mind initially, because my husband, Dave, is a champion "care caster." It says, "Casting the whole of your care [all your anxieties, all your worries, all your concerns, once and for all] on Him, for

He cares for you affectionately *and* cares about you watchfully" (AMPC). That's good news— news that Dave understood and lived by long before I did.

I was a worrier for years, but as I began to walk with God, I learned that worry, anxiety, and care literally have no positive effect on our lives. They never bring a solution to problems, and they prevent our spiritual growth. With this in mind, let's think about the story Jesus told in Mark

> *Worry is caused by not trusting God to take care of the various situations we face.*

4:1–19. He talked about a farmer who sowed seed in different types of soil, which produced different kinds of results. When He explained this parable, He compared the seed to the Word of God that is planted in our hearts. He said in Mark 4:19 that "the worries of this life" can "choke the word, making it unfruitful." In other words, when we worry, God's Word does not bring forth the blessings He intends it to produce in our lives.

I believe that trying to burden us with cares and concerns is one of the primary ways Satan tries to steal the Word of God from the hearts of committed Christians and keep them focused on their troubles instead of resting in God's goodness. As women, we need our hearts to be free to meditate on God's Word. Our families need us to be women of the Word so we can receive revelation about how we are to live, both individually and as a family unit. Our employers need us to be women of the Word so they can trust and depend on our God-given wisdom, integrity, and understanding. Our churches need us to be women of the Word so we can help meet the needs of others within the church and in our communities.

These good things only come when God's truths are rooted in our hearts. Philippians 4:6 reminds us not to "be anxious about anything, but *in every situation*, by prayer and petition, with thanksgiving, present your requests to God" (italics mine). The instruction is clear: We are not to allow ourselves to be weighed down and distracted by worry. The reason for this is what we learned in Mark 4:19—that when our minds are constantly on ourselves, our problems, and our personal needs, we become ineffective and powerless.

We need to develop the habit of praying about everything and worrying about nothing. When we worry, it indicates that we think we can solve our problems by ourselves. And although women can handle and manage a lot, we are not built to handle our problems. God created us to be dependent upon Him and to give the challenges and difficulties of our lives to Him and allow Him to help us with them.

The only way to have victory in our lives is to play by God's rules, and He says we must stop worrying if we want to have peace. When we face situations that cause us to be concerned, we need God's help. The way to get His help is to do as Philippians 4:6 and 1 Peter 5:7 teach us: stop worrying, pray, humble ourselves, and cast our cares on Him. Instead of making ourselves miserable trying to figure out what to do in the circumstances that cause us to fret, God wants us to place our trust in Him and enter into His rest, totally abandoning ourselves to His care. This seems clear and simple, yet many women today continue to struggle because we are accustomed to doing so much for ourselves and for others that we can be reluctant to ask for help.

When we learn to ask God for His help and lean on Him in trust, our lives begin to change. But as long as we try to handle things ourselves, God will let us. He will not take care of our problems and worries—our cares—until we release them and give them to Him. This doesn't mean that we are to become irresponsible or lazy.

God will not do for us what we can do for ourselves. We must do what we can do and then
trust God to do what we cannot do. When
we humble ourselves and
ask for His help, then He
releases His power in our
situations.

> *When we learn to ask God for His help and lean on Him in trust, our lives begin to change.*

Let me ask you some
questions that just might
inspire you to make some changes that will
benefit you: Can you imagine your life without
worry? How much more freedom, happiness,
and fulfillment would you enjoy if you were
not worried about things? Why not start today
to live a worry-free life? Ask God to show you
every time you are taking on care instead of
casting it off. When He makes you aware of
it, be willing to immediately release it to Him.
He wants you to develop the habit of casting
all your care on Him because He cares for you.

Habit Builders

When anxiety was great within me,
your consolation brought me joy.

Psalm 94:19

Do not let your hearts be troubled
(distressed, agitated). You believe in *and*
adhere to *and* trust in *and* rely on God;
believe in *and* adhere to *and*
trust in *and* rely also on Me.

John 14:1 AMPC

Therefore I tell you, stop being
perpetually uneasy (anxious and worried)
about your life, what you shall eat *or
what you shall drink*; or about your body,
what you shall put on. Is not life greater
[in quality] than food, and the body [far
above and more excellent] than clothing?

Look at the birds of the air; they neither sow nor reap nor gather into barns, and yet your heavenly Father keeps feeding them. Are you not worth much more than they? And who of you by worrying *and* being anxious can add one unit of measure (cubit) to his stature *or* to the span of his life?

Matthew 6:25–27 AMPC

CHAPTER 18

The Habit of Generosity

We make a living by what we get, but we make a life by what we give.

—Winston Churchill

Have you ever considered the fact that it's possible to develop a habit of generosity? Some people are generous to certain people on certain occasions, perhaps birthdays or Christmas, but at other times they simply don't think about being generous. They are not looking for opportunities to give to others, seeking to do something extra or unexpected for someone, or finding ways to be generous to people they may not even know. I believe forming a habit of generosity honors God because He is generous in every way, toward everyone. I once heard that when we give, we are more like God than at any other time, and one way we can show our appreciation for everything God has done for us is to be a blessing to others.

When we have established habits in our lives, we miss them when we are not doing them. I hope the habit of generosity will become so ingrained in you that if you go too long without doing something for others, you begin to yearn and look for ways to be kind to them. For years, it never occurred to me to be generous to others, but now I purposefully try to find out how I can bless people. I make a point to know what people need and want and ask the Holy Spirit to lead me in meeting their needs through me as He sees fit. I am quick to say that some of the greatest joys in my life have come from being a blessing to others.

To be generous means to choose to do more than we feel we have to do and to always do as much for others as we possibly can. It means that we are aware of and sensitive to other people's needs and desires, and we are eager to meet those needs to the greatest possible degree. A generous person truly cares about others and looks for ways to bless them on purpose, with no strings attached.

> *To be generous means to choose to do more than we feel we have to do and to always do as much for others as we possibly can.*

People who give grudgingly or expect something in return do not express true generosity. But those who give from a willing heart, simply wanting to bless others, express the type of generosity God wants us to show. As 2 Corinthians 9:7 says, He "loves a *cheerful* giver" (italics mine).

Many times, generosity involves a financial blessing, but we can also be generous with our time, our gifts and talents, our professional skills, our friendship, and our willingness to help others in whatever ways they need help. If you are in a tight place right now and don't have much money to give to others, don't let the enemy convince you that you cannot develop the habit of generosity. You have something wonderful to offer the people around you, whether it's being able to sew or clean house, making a delicious cup of coffee and taking a few minutes to have a friend into your home to catch up, being a good listener to someone who is struggling and needs to talk, or cleaning out your cupboards or jewelry box and giving away items you no longer use. You may know how to dress nicely on a budget or how to apply makeup in flattering ways, and there may be someone around you who wants to learn how to present herself better. You may be a retired person who has years of experience in a certain industry, and you could be generous with the lessons you have learned so that you can help a young person just starting out in the same career.

There are so many ways to be generous, and true generosity is a matter of the heart. Second Corinthians 8:12 says, "For if the willingness is there, the gift is acceptable according to what one has, not according to what one does not have."

If you'll ask God to show you how He wants you to express generosity to bless others, He will, and you will find great joy in doing it.

A spirit of generosity inspires a person to give when giving doesn't seem to make sense or when giving requires stretching beyond what is comfortable. The ancient church of Macedonia provides a good example of this. The believers there were suffering greatly and experiencing severe lack, yet they had so much joy in God that they felt compelled to give abundantly. According to 2 Corinthians 8:2–3, they didn't stop at giving only what they could afford; they gave sacrificially. Simply thinking about this story makes me admire these people and want to live with the same attitude they demonstrated. Generous people are attractive. Others are drawn to them and enjoy being around them as much as possible, while no one wants to be in the presence of someone stingy or greedy for very long.

Greed and self-focus seem to be increasing in our society today. Nothing good comes from greedy, self-absorbed people. The opposite of greed is generosity, and nothing combats the negativity of focusing on ourselves more than doing something for someone else. The more we grow in godliness, the less we think about ourselves and the more interested we become in other people. We can learn to get up every day with the goal of intentionally being a blessing to someone. I actually believe that one of the primary

> *The more we grow in godliness, the less we think about ourselves and the more interested we become in other people.*

themes of our lives as godly women should be giving, serving, and loving others. Philippians 2:3–4 says, "Let each regard the others as better than *and* superior to himself [thinking more highly of one another than you do of yourselves]. Let each of you esteem *and* look upon *and* be concerned for not [merely] his own interests, but also each for the interests of others" (AMPC).

Maybe you are now like I was years ago, and the idea of developing the habit of generosity simply isn't something that occurs to you often. Maybe you are busy trying to make ends meet each month, and sometimes there's more month than there is money. I understand that. But I also know that if you have a heart to become a generous person, God will give you ways to do it. My prayer for you echoes Paul's prayer for the believers in Corinth, that "you will be enriched in every way so that you can be generous on every occasion" (2 Cor. 9:11).

Habit Builders

Good will come to those who are
generous and lend freely, who conduct
their affairs with justice.

Psalm 112:5

One person gives freely, yet gains
even more; another withholds unduly,
but comes to poverty. A generous person
will prosper; whoever refreshes
others will be refreshed.

Proverbs 11:24–25

Give, and it will be given to you. A good
measure, pressed down, shaken together
and running over, will be poured into
your lap. For with the measure you use,
it will be measured to you."

Luke 6:38

CHAPTER 19

The Habit of Confidence

For the Spirit God gave us does not make us timid, but gives us power, love and self-discipline.

—2 Timothy 1:7

Developing confidence can make every area of your life better. It makes difficult things easier because it causes you to believe you can overcome them, and it makes you feel better about who you are and what you can do. I'm not talking about the kind of confidence the world gives, but about confidence in God. I define this kind of confidence as the belief that you are capable and able to do whatever needs to be done because God gives you strength to do it. I have also referred to it in various teachings as "godly assertiveness" and as the expectation that you will succeed in whatever God leads you to do. A confident person's attitude is steadfast, fearless, and strong in the Lord, and it is full of *cans*, not *can'ts*.

For the first forty years or so of my life, I was insecure and lacked confidence. But as I learned to walk with God and live according to His Word, I became a confident person. If I were to look for confidence in myself, I would be disappointed often, but if my confidence is in Christ, I can rest assured that He will empower me to do whatever I need to do in any situation.

One of my favorite Scriptures about confidence is Philippians 4:13. It doesn't specifically use the word *confidence*, but it helps us understand exactly what confidence in God is and how it works: "I have strength for all things in Christ Who empowers me [I am ready for anything and equal to anything through Him Who infuses inner strength into me; I am self-sufficient in Christ's sufficiency]" (AMPC).

I have found that confidence is also a choice. A part of that choice is deciding to believe God's Word, such as Philippians 4:13, other verses mentioned in this chapter, and the ones listed as Habit Builders at the end of this chapter. Some women come across as timid, insecure, or filled with doubt. Regardless of the life experiences or innate temperaments that cause them to act this way, they can overcome these things by choosing to become confident and walking with God as He strengthens them. God wants us to be bold and confident in Him. It's a gift from God that everyone can decide to walk in or not and a habit we can choose to develop. It's not a feeling; it's a deliberate mindset.

Sometimes when I am ministering to crowds of people, I don't necessarily feel confident, so I have to decide to be confident. I cannot always discern whether people are interested in what I am saying or not. If I were to let that affect my level of confidence, I would be tossed about emotionally in many directions. The same principle is true for you: You may not speak to an audience of thousands, but you certainly have other people in your life. If you allow them or the way they respond to you to determine whether you are confident or not, then you will continually require a fresh "fix" of approving nods, glances, or words. The acceptance other people offer us feels good for a season, but it's not enough to carry us through life. God can certainly use their affirmation to bless us, but He does not want us to find our confidence and strength in it.

> *The acceptance other people offer us feels good for a season, but it's not enough to carry us through life.*

True confidence starts in the soul and works from the inside out. It starts in our hearts and minds and then enables us to do what we would not be able to do if we felt insecure or if we lacked courage and strength. A person's real life—who they truly are—is on the inside, not the outside. It has nothing to do with what they own or what they do for a living or how highly educated or talented they are. These things may help describe a person, but they are not the most important aspects of anyone's life.

There are many people in the world who work to project an attitude of confidence and strength, but they are miserable inside. Real confidence is not some kind of feeling people work up so they can go into the world and move fast and talk loud and act as though they are stronger or more capable than others.

In contrast, a person who has the confidence that comes from God is at peace in her soul, and she walks in humility, knowing that He is the source of her strength and that everything she does, she does by His grace. Jesus said in John 15:5 that we can do nothing apart from Him. A person of real confidence knows this is true and relies on the Holy Spirit for the courage and ability to do whatever she needs to do. A woman of genuine confidence never has to try to sell herself to others or convince them she is capable of doing great things. She simply does what needs to be done and trusts God with her reputation. The Lord will cause others to recognize her abilities, if and when that needs to happen. She knows that godly assertiveness is a quiet and beautiful quality that begins in the heart, and she stands firm in the conviction that she is not alone, that God is with her, and that she is able to do whatever she needs to do.

> *A woman of genuine confidence never has to try to sell herself to others or convince them she is capable of doing great things.*

I want to encourage you to commit to building the habit of confidence. It will make such a positive difference in your life. Choose to believe and say "I can" instead of "I can't," knowing that God's Word promises you can do all things that are within His will, through Christ because He gives you strength (Phil. 4:13). Put your trust in His ability to work through you, not in what you think you can do on your own. Romans 8:31 says, "If God is for us, who can be against us?" As a believer, you can trust that God is for you. He is on your side. He fights your battles, and whatever battle He fights, He wins. He is always leading you in triumph in Christ (2 Cor. 2:14). Every morning when you wake up, believe you will succeed in every situation, and tell yourself, "God has something good for me today!"

Habit Builders

The effect of righteousness will be peace,
and the result of righteousness will be
quietness and confident trust forever.

Isaiah 32:17 AMP

Blessed is the one who trusts in the LORD,
whose confidence is in him.

Jeremiah 17:7

Let us then approach God's throne
of grace with confidence,
so that we may receive mercy
and find grace to help us
in our time of need.

Hebrews 4:16

CHAPTER 20
The Habit of Simplicity

The more you have, the more you are occupied.
The less you have, the freer you are.

—Mother Teresa of Calcutta

In today's busy and complicated world, have you discovered that trying to keep things simple can be a real challenge? Even things we think *should* be simple can quickly become complicated for various reasons. We sometimes think, *I'll just run to the store for a gallon of milk.* But when we get there, we realize we also need eggs, juice, and bread. Then we remember that one family member likes apple juice while another likes orange juice and struggle to remember which one we're running low on. When we call home to find out, the person who answers the phone says, "And can you also get some cereal? I don't like the brand you got last week, so can you get something else...And on your way home can you pick up the dry cleaning? I forgot that I need my gray sweater tomorrow, and it's at the cleaners." By the time we leave the supermarket, we have a whole shopping cart full of groceries, and we may have talked to every member of the family, expressing preferences and opinions—all for what we thought was one gallon of milk.

Some people have the innate ability to complicate even the simplest things. There was a time in my life when I made everything much more complicated than it needed to be. I seemed to be able to complicate the simplest situations. Once I became a Christian, I began to realize that this area of my life needed some serious attention. I didn't like complicating things, and I didn't intend to make them more difficult than they should have been, and yet I kept doing it.

When I looked at the people around me, especially other women at a similar stage of life, my world seemed so much more complex than theirs. Every area of my life seemed to be complicated—not only my actions but also my thought processes. I even complicated my relationship with God because I had developed a legalistic approach to righteousness. To me, life itself was complicated. I felt that I had a lot of complex problems, and I didn't realize they were that way only because of my convoluted approach to life. Eventually I learned that when we are complicated inside, everything else in our lives seems complicated, too.

Many times the act of complicating situations is born out of an unhealthy need to impress people. Because I was abused in my childhood, I felt very insecure about myself for many years. People who are insecure try to impress others because they feel they might not be accepted if they act like who they really are.

I remember a good example of one way I used to complicate things. Entertaining friends and guests in our home was something I always wanted to do but never really enjoyed. I could make plans for a simple hamburger and hot dog barbecue with my husband, Dave, and three other couples and, before the gathering was over, turn it into a nightmare.

> *When we are complicated inside, everything else in our lives seems complicated, too.*

Because of my insecurities, when I entertained, everything had to be perfect—just the right food and drinks, an immaculate house, manicured yard, and spotless lawn furniture. All the children had to look like they just stepped out of a fashion magazine, and of course I had to wear just the right outfit, and every single hair had to be in place.

And because I was afraid someone might feel left out, I would end up inviting several more couples than I had originally planned to include—which meant there might not be enough lawn chairs outside for everyone. So I would rush out to buy more chairs, for which we really didn't have the money.

Somewhere along the way, I would decide to change the simple plan for hot dogs and hamburgers, baked beans, and potato chips to a menu I felt was more impressive. So I would rush to the grocery store and buy steaks that we couldn't afford, and make potato salad, which was a two-hour project, and prepare enough additional side dishes to feed a small army—because I could not bear the thought of running out of food and spoiling my image! I could have just made iced tea, coffee, and lemonade, but I had to have all of those, plus four kinds of soda pop.

I worked so hard before the event started that I was worn out by the time our guests arrived. Even their arrival did not put an end to my labor. I continued to work most of the time they were there—setting out and putting away food, washing dishes, and cleaning the kitchen.

Then I would feel resentment building in my heart because it seemed that everyone else was having fun and enjoying themselves and leaving all the work to me. By the time the evening was over, I was worn out both physically and mentally—wondering how a simple get-together had ballooned into such a major production.

Finally I had to face the truth about my insecurities and admit that my need for admiration and acceptance was creating the problem. When I sought God's help, I began to

understand that in order to have a simpler life
that I could enjoy, I would have to change. Life
was not going to change; I had to change.

Can you relate to my story about the barbecue? Does it describe your approach to life?
Maybe you have done the very things I did, or
maybe you go through something similar when
you are preparing to host out-of-town guests
or when you are in charge of a church or community event or when making an important
work presentation. Proverbs 16:3 gives good
instruction to women like I once was, who
tend to complicate everything: "Commit to the
LORD whatever you do, and he will establish
your plans."

God eventually helped me see that there is
no need for me to make a project out of every
event in my life. Once I understood *why* I
always wanted everything to be perfect, I was
able to deal with my insecurities and come into

agreement with the easy, peaceful, joy-filled way God wants us to live. It didn't happen overnight—it was a process—but eventually I was able to relax and start simplifying my life.

I have a revelation for you: Simplicity brings joy, while complication steals joy. If you are a woman who complicates life as I did, you too can commit your complicated works to the Lord. You can come into agreement with the way He wants you to live, and you can enjoy everything you do. Life doesn't have to be full

> *Simplicity brings joy, while complication steals joy.*

of complicated events, so just relax, develop the habit of keeping things simple, trust God, and let Him establish your plans.

Habit Builders

Take delight in the LORD, and he will
give you the desires of your heart.
Commit your way to the LORD;
trust in him and he will do this.

Psalm 37:4–5

Better one handful with tranquility
than two handfuls with toil
and chasing after the wind.

Ecclesiastes 4:6

Those who live according to the flesh have
their minds set on what the flesh desires;
but those who live in accordance with
the Spirit have their minds set on what
the Spirit desires. The mind governed by
the flesh is death, but the mind governed
by the Spirit is life and peace.

Romans 8:5–6

CHAPTER 21

The Habit of Serving Others

Lose no occasion of serving God. And since he is invisible to our eyes, we are to serve him in our neighbor; which he receives as if done to himself in person, standing visibly before us.

—John Wesley

Servants and martyrs both do things for people, but they do them with very different attitudes rooted in different motives. We all know what a martyr is. We've heard the stories of heroic men and women who, down through the ages, have paid the ultimate price and given their lives for what they believed in. But there's another kind of martyr—one without courage or nobility. Some women are especially prone to the kind of martyr-like behavior I'm talking about, and I'm sure we all know one—a great and constant sufferer who thrives on sharing her pain and struggles with anyone who will listen. This martyr wants everyone around to know the sacrifices she is making in life.

I once knew a woman like this. She felt like a slave to her family, and she definitely had the attitude of a martyr. Frankly, I grew tired of hearing her continually talk about how much she did for everyone and how little anyone appreciated her—and so did other people. I could tell she kept a running account of what she was doing for them versus what they were doing for her. Eventually she succeeded in ruining her marriage and most of her relationships with her children. What a tragedy.

The martyr trap is an easy one to fall into.

It's so easy and can seem so natural for women to start out serving their families and friends—and loving it. After all, that's what much of society says women are supposed to do. We tend to put duty to others before our own ambitions. We are the caretakers, the peacemakers, the ones who assure our family members that we are always there for them and that everything will be all right. We often make sure everyone gets fed and has clean clothes. We may make sure the

> *The martyr trap is an easy one to fall into.*

coffee pot at work never runs dry and be the first to volunteer to meet a need in our church or community.

After a while, however, our hearts may begin to change, and we begin to expect something in return for all the effort and care we are expending. After all, we're working so hard and sacrificing so much. Eventually we no longer have the heart of a servant. We become discouraged because our expectations aren't being met. We resent what we do for others, and our attitude goes sour, and soon we find we've become mired in self-pity. We've become martyrs. I know—I've been there.

One morning as I got up and went downstairs to make coffee, I felt the Lord encouraging me to prepare a fruit salad for Dave. He loves fruit salad in the morning, and I knew it would be a nice gesture for me to make one for him. He wasn't up yet, and I had time to prepare it, so I could surprise him with it when he came downstairs.

The problem was, I didn't want to make him a fruit salad. I could have handled putting a banana or an apple on a plate, but I didn't want to take the time and effort to cut up all the fruit and put it in a bowl and serve it to him. I wanted to pray and read my Bible instead. I thought, *Why do I always have to do this stuff for him? Why doesn't he do things for me? After*

*all, I have to study the Bible and pray. That's my
ministry!*

It's funny how we sometimes make the mistake of thinking that religious works somehow
take the place of true obedience and make us
more holy, but they don't. That day the Lord
patiently reminded me that serving Dave in this
way was actually serving Him. It was putting
into action the Bible that I loved to read. So I
obediently made the fruit salad and surprised
Dave with it when he came downstairs—and I
had peace with God because I knew I had done
what He wanted me to do.

I wonder how many marriages could be
saved from divorce courts if the partners were
willing to show love by serving one another
instead of trying to get their spouses to serve
them? How many people could be happy at
work, instead of miserable, if people on the
same team were not competing but helping
each other succeed? It seems that everyone

today wants to be free—and Jesus has indeed set us free. However, He never intended for that freedom to be used for selfish purposes. Galatians 5:13 says, "You…were [indeed] called to freedom; only [do not let your] freedom be an incentive to your flesh *and* an opportunity *or* excuse [for selfishness], but through love you should serve one another" (AMPC). This verse confirms that God wants us to be servants.

I definitely love my husband. I could say "I love you" twenty times a day, but sometimes that love is best expressed through service. Words are wonderful, but when we walk in love, our commitment contains much more than words. How can I truly love my husband if I never want to do anything for him?

I don't recall getting any particular reward the morning I made Dave's fruit salad. He did thank me, but nothing spectacular occurred as a result of that act of kindness. However, I'm sure that God rewarded me that day with peace and joy and a sense of His presence. I am sure that He also arranged for someone to do something for me, something that person would not have done had I not sown that seed of obedience.

Jesus spoke some powerful words, which are commonly called the Golden Rule, when He said, "So in everything, do to others what you would have them do to you" (Matt. 7:12). I'm sure that we women have missed out on blessings we've never even known about simply because we failed to do for others what we would have liked someone to have done for us. We want the people we bless to bless us in return, but it doesn't always work that way. We should do everything we do as though we are doing it to serve and honor the Lord, and then look to Him for our reward.

> *We should do everything we do as though we are doing it to serve and honor the Lord, and then look to Him for our reward.*

If your marriage, family, or some other relationship in your life isn't what you would like it to be, you could turn it around by adopting this one principle right now. You may have been waiting for your husband or a friend to do something for you. Maybe you have even been stubbornly refusing to be the first to make a move. I encourage you to swallow your pride and save your relationship. Stop being a martyr who is always talking about all the sacrifices you make. Begin to walk in true love and humility by serving others. Make them the focus, not yourself. By developing the habit of being obedient to God's call to serve Him by serving the people around you, you will not only bless others, but you will be blessed as well. And, if you are worried about being taken advantage of, you don't need to be. God will always take care of you if you serve others because of your love for Him.

Habit Builders

Therefore, my dear brothers and sisters,
stand firm. Let nothing move you.
Always give yourselves fully to the work
of the Lord, because you know that your
labor in the Lord is not in vain.

1 Corinthians 15:58

You, my brothers and sisters, were called
to be free. But do not use your freedom
to indulge the flesh; rather,
serve one another humbly in love.

Galatians 5:13

Each of you should use whatever gift
you have received to serve others,
as faithful stewards of God's grace
in its various forms.

1 Peter 4:10

CHAPTER 22

The Habit of Contentment

A harvest of peace grows from seeds of contentment.

—Indian proverb

A woman who has formed the habit of being content is a joy to be around. Think about it: How much do you enjoy someone who constantly complains about her life and is never satisfied? Not much! But a woman who is thankful for what she does have and satisfied with the life God has given her is an inspiration and a good example to others. Being content does not mean never wanting anything.

It simply means you don't become obsessed with wanting something to the point where you think, *I can never be happy until I have such-and-such.*

To be content is to recognize God's goodness in your life, to realize that He always wants you in the right circumstances at the right time, and that He will give you the blessings you can handle. It doesn't mean you have no hope or vision for your life to get better, but it means you do not allow the things you do not have to keep you from enjoying what you do have. When I write about things we do not have, I am not simply talking about material things, such as a nice car or nice clothes. I am talking about anything we may wish for,

> *To be content is to recognize God's goodness in your life, to realize that He always wants you in the right circumstances at the right time, and that He will give you the blessings you can handle.*

including things like certain relationships, job opportunities, an increased level of influence, skills or talents, or experiences in life. A contented woman trusts God in all things, at all times, as I wrote about in the chapter on trusting God.

Earlier in my life, I went through quite a few years of being very frustrated, and part of my problem was that I did not know how to enjoy where I was on the way to where I was going. God always calls us forward and desires increase in our lives, but He wants us to trust Him for the right timing and He wants us to live at peace and with joy while we wait. God has a wonderful plan for our lives and it unfolds progressively. We don't have to wait until we have the end result to enjoy where we are and be content. We can find our satisfaction in Him while we are on our way to the fulfillment of our hopes and dreams.

Ecclesiastes 6:9 says, "Better is the sight of the

eyes [the enjoyment of what is available to one] than the cravings of wandering desire. This is also vanity (emptiness, falsity, and futility) and a striving after the wind *and* a feeding on it" (AMPC). The writer of this passage (believed to be Solomon) is saying that an obsessive desire for something we do not have is pointless and useless and that the best way to live is to enjoy what is already available to us.

The apostle Paul wrote that he had "learned to be content whatever the circumstances," and we should aspire to do this too (Phil. 4:11). Many times, when people talk about this verse, they focus on the word *content*. But I believe the word *learned* is just as important. We have to learn to be content; it doesn't automatically happen to us when we become a Christian.

I don't know about you, but as I mentioned earlier in this chapter, it took many years before I learned contentment, even as a believer. I believe many other women struggle as I did, trying to find it. You may be one of them. I knew how to be satisfied if I was getting my own way—if everything was working exactly as I had planned—but how often does that happen? Very rarely, in my experience. I knew absolutely nothing about how to handle even the ordinary trials that come along in almost every woman's life. I didn't know how to adapt to other people and to changing situations.

I found out that a woman who can only be satisfied when there are no disturbances in life will spend much of her time being discontented. Eventually, I came to desire stability so much that I was willing to learn whatever it took to have it. I wanted to be *content* no matter what was going on in my life.

A woman who can only be satisfied when there are no disturbances in life will spend much of her time being discontented.

The Amplified Bible, Classic Edition amplifies the word *content* in Philippians 4:11 this way: "satisfied to the point where I am not disturbed or disquieted." I appreciate this definition because it does not say that we should be satisfied to the point where we don't ever want change, but that we can be satisfied to the point that we are not anxious or disturbed.

Many women today find themselves dissatisfied, and then they begin *looking for contentment in all the wrong places*. For years I looked for contentment and satisfaction in material things and work-related success. The result was that I never found it. I was never truly satisfied. We usually blame our discontentment on someone or something. I often thought that if Dave would change and do more of what I wanted him to do, I would be content. But no matter what he did, it wasn't enough. He eventually told me that he finally realized that no matter what he did, he could never satisfy me, so he was going to quit working so hard at it. I also thought that I would be content if my ministry would grow. But even when it did grow, I still found myself discontent.

The prophet Jeremiah compares looking for satisfaction in all the wrong places to digging empty wells that have no water in them (Jer. 2:13). The answer to my constant frustration came when I received the revelation that my satisfaction had to be in Jesus Christ. I came to know what a privilege it was to live under His guidance, trusting that He would never fail me.

When Paul said he had learned to be content, he was saying that even if he did not particularly like the situation in which he found himself, he still trusted God. Therefore, his trust kept him in perfect peace.

When our minds are focused on the presence of God and His goodness in our lives, we are content and peaceful (Isa. 26:3). What God offers us is better than anything the world has to give. He is our greatest treasure, and nothing compares to knowing Him and experiencing His love and guidance each day. If you know God, you have everything. You can trust Him to meet your needs and to know the desires of your heart. You can rest and learn to develop the habit of contentment in Him.

Habit Builders

Trust in the Lord and do good;
dwell in the land and enjoy safe pasture.
Take delight in the Lord, and he will
give you the desires of your heart.

Psalm 37:3–4

But seek first his kingdom and
his righteousness, and all these things
will be given to you as well.

Matthew 6:33

And my God will meet all your needs
according to the riches of his glory
in Christ Jesus.

Philippians 4:19

Keep your lives free from the love
of money and be content with
what you have, because God has said,
"Never will I leave you;
never will I forsake you."

Hebrews 13:5

CHAPTER 23

The Habit of Excellence

We are what we repeatedly do. Excellence, then, is not an act, but a habit.

—Aristotle

A godly woman forms the habit of being excellent in all she does, even in a world full of mediocrity. Excellence is an aspect of all that God calls us to be, and it sets believers apart from the world in a positive way. God Himself is excellent, and according to Genesis 1:27, we are created in His image, so it is important for us to strive to be excellent, too. In fact, to reach our full potential in Him and to fulfill

His purpose for our lives, we will need to be excellent.

It's easy to think of being excellent in terms of our actions. And it's true: We demonstrate excellence by doing things well. But excellence begins in our hearts; it's an attitude. One of the people in the Bible who demonstrates this is Daniel. According to Daniel 5:12, Daniel had "an excellent spirit" (AMPC). If we don't have an excellent spirit (meaning an attitude of excellence), we will compromise on many things and be content with mediocrity. Choose to be excellent, to go the extra mile and do everything you do the very best that you can, and do it to honor God.

Excellence is an extremely high-quality virtue to be pursued. It means doing more than we have to do to get by or doing something better than is necessary. It also means doing the very best

> *Excellence begins in our hearts; it's an attitude.*

we can in every situation, but it does *not* mean perfection. It's important to make this distinction, because many women have the tendency to be perfectionists. Perfectionism leads to frustration and causes people to feel they have failed when they do not achieve it. But excellence feels empowering and rewarding.

To begin to develop the habit of excellence, I would encourage you to be aware of mediocrity so you can always go beyond it. For example, it's easy to sweep the middle of a room, but to be excellent you sweep under the edges of the counters and under the furniture, too. It is easy to be late for an appointment and not consider how your tardiness affects the person waiting for you. It's also easy to quickly fill out an expense report at work and turn it in to the accounting office, thinking they will check the math, but an excellent person verifies that everything is in order and properly documented, and double-checks to make sure the addition is correct. God has not called us to take the easy path. He has called us to be excellent.

I also believe it's helpful when you are developing the habit of excellence to come up with some kind of system that reminds you to break through your comfort zone or go beyond what is mediocre. I like to make notes or signs to remind me of certain things sometimes. As you are developing the habit of excellence, you might want to simply write the word *excellence* on a sticky note and post it in strategic places. That one word will be enough to remind you of what you need to do.

I am also a proponent of spoken confessions. You might consider saying aloud multiple times each day, "I do everything I do with excellence." After doing this for a while, you could expand it and say, "I take excellent care of myself and the people in my family," or "I steward the resources God has given me with excellence," or "I do excellent work at my job." You are aware of the various areas of your life, so you can think of the confessions that will be most effective for you. Habits are developed through repetition, so the more you practice excellence, the more ingrained the habit of excellence will become in you.

An important part of being excellent involves the way we treat other people. We can be excellent in all other areas of our lives—we do not leave a speck of dust anywhere when we clean the house, or we perform every aspect of our jobs with integrity and to the highest standards, or we continually go above and beyond the call of duty to carry out any task we face better than anyone else—but we are not truly excellent if we treat others poorly. We may fail at times and fall short of God's standard of love. We are not

> *An important part of being excellent involves the way we treat other people.*

perfect and we will not love perfectly; only God can do that. But we can have a heart to love others excellently, and God will honor it.

There is no one on earth that God does not value. He made all people, and He loves each one and does not take kindly to seeing anyone mistreated. Out of reverence to Him, we should be polite, respectful, and appreciative toward everyone. We should also look for something to affirm in the people around us and find some way to encourage them. Everyone wants to feel valuable and loved, and many people wrestle with feelings of low self-worth. As godly women, we have the power of the Holy Spirit inside of us and we have the love of God in our hearts (Rom. 5:5), so we have the ability to express love to others.

The apostle Paul understood love and wrote what is referred to as "the love chapter" of the Bible, 1 Corinthians 13. In the beginning of that chapter, he basically says that he could do everything in the world better than anyone else and to the farthest extreme, but without love in his heart, none of it would matter. That's the way I feel about the habits in this book. You can be great at all of them. You can do them better than everyone else, but if they are not motivated by love, they are simply good practices. They do have some practical value on their own, but they take on a whole new level of purpose and joy when they are done in love. To make the most of each one, make sure you do it with a heart of love for God and for people.

According to the apostle Paul, love is the most excellent way to live: "But earnestly desire *and* zealously cultivate the greatest *and* best gifts *and* graces (the higher gifts and the choicest graces). And yet I will show you a still more excellent way [one that is better by far and the highest of them all—love]" (1 Cor. 12:31 AMPC). When we love others, we can be assured that we are living the most excellent way.

Habit Builders

And this I pray, that your love may abound
still more and more in knowledge
and all discernment, that you may approve
the things that are excellent, that you
may be sincere and without offense
till the day of Christ.

Philippians 1:9–10 NKJV

Finally, brothers and sisters, whatever
is true, whatever is noble, whatever is
right, whatever is pure, whatever is lovely,
whatever is admirable—if anything
is excellent or praiseworthy—
think about such things.

Philippians 4:8

Whatever you do, work at it with
all your heart, as working for the Lord,
not for human masters.

Colossians 3:23

CHAPTER 24

The Habit of Discipline and Self-Control

For the Spirit God gave us does not make us timid, but gives us power, love and self-discipline.

—2 Timothy 1:7

A. B. Simpson writes in his book *The Gentle Love of the Holy Spirit* that "temperance which is discipline and self-control is true self-love, and the proper regard for our real interests, which is as much the duty of love as is regard for the interests of others."

If we fail to take care of ourselves, we won't be able to help and take care of others. The best gift you can give your family and friends is a healthy you, and a healthy you will require discipline. Work is good for us, but it must be balanced with plenty of good rest and quality sleep. We need to eat healthy foods; drink plenty of good, clean water; get adequate exercise; laugh and have fun; and eliminate excess stress from our lives. I didn't always do this, and I eventually became very sick. But thankfully, I learned from my bad habits, and now I work smarter, not harder. I accomplish a lot, but I do it at a pace that is healthy for me, while taking time to also enjoy the life that God has given to me.

I have had to break bad habits and build good habits many times in my life. I know from experience that the process of replacing ungodly habits with godly ones is not easy. I want to be a great encourager to you as you develop the habits of a godly woman, but I also want you to know that I understand that doing so may be difficult at times. Some new habits seem to come easily for some people, and I hope some will come easily for you. Other habits are challenging to develop. Many godly habits come primarily through discipline and self-control, along with the help of the Holy Spirit.

Discipline and self-control are not always popular concepts because they require us to give up something—perhaps free time, relaxation, or something we think is fun even though we know it isn't good for us. But discipline and self-control also give us something. They benefit us by helping us incorporate good qualities and attitudes into our lives, and they are essential if we want to develop the habits of a godly woman. The habits of discipline and self-control make all other good habits possible, because habits rarely just happen. They

develop as we practice them over and over
again.

Hebrews 12:11 teaches us that "no discipline seems pleasant at the time, but painful. Later on, however, it produces a harvest
of righteousness and
peace for those who
have been trained by
it." Even the writer of
Hebrews understood
that discipline is not
something that makes us feel joyful. The fact
of the matter is, it's hard! But it leads to something wonderful. I'm sure you've heard the old
saying "No pain, no gain." And it's true. When
we want something worth having, we almost
always have to work at it.

> *The habits of discipline
> and self-control make
> all other good habits
> possible, because habits
> rarely just happen.*

Three verses in John 14 are very helpful for
anyone who desires to develop godly habits and
is willing to make the efforts needed to do so.
In John 14:16–17, Jesus says, "And I will ask

the Father, and he will give you another advocate to help you and be with you forever—the Spirit of truth. The world cannot accept him, because it neither sees him nor knows him. But you know him, for he lives with you and will be in you." In John 14:26, Jesus says, "But the Advocate, the Holy Spirit, whom the Father will send in my name, will teach you all things and will remind you of everything I have said to you." Jesus' words assure us that the Holy Spirit will help us do everything God asks us to do. If we are doing our best to develop godly habits, we can count on Him to help us in every way. We do need to have a desire and make an effort to be disciplined and to exercise self-control, but we do not have to do anything alone. He is always with us to guide and empower us.

Although the idea of discipline does not make us happy initially, it is intended to produce joy ultimately. God wants us to be happy and enjoy our lives. I have come to believe that we will not be truly happy or really enjoy our lives if we are not committed to discipline and self-control. Just think about some of the unhappiest people you know and ask yourself if they are disciplined people or if they know how to control themselves. The answer to both questions is probably no. Many times, unhappy people feel bad about themselves and pressured by feelings of frustration, failure, or guilt. They almost always have bad habits. When I think of them, I feel compassion, and I think that surely it would have been better for them in the long run to go through the pain of becoming disciplined than to have remained unhappy for years due to negative or destructive habits. Perhaps some of those people wish that they had taken the time and energy necessary to build good habits.

I have heard plenty of people say, "I'm just not a disciplined person," or "I need to be more disciplined." Discipline never comes by wishing for it, but through the willingness to go through a process that may be difficult or painful in order to get from a negative place to a good place. Paul told Timothy that God has given us a spirit of discipline and self-control (2 Tim. 1:7 AMPC). But there is a difference between having something and using it. Start by believing that you have discipline and self-control in you, and then work with the Holy Spirit to develop it and incorporate it into your life.

I am writing honestly about discipline and self-control in this chapter and attempting to be straightforward about the fact that they are not easy. I also want to encourage you not to dwell on the difficulty of forming a new habit, but to focus on the joy and freedom that will come as that habit gets ingrained in your daily routine and in your life. Remember, as I mentioned in the introduction to this book, it takes twenty-one to thirty days to develop a new habit. I would suggest that you not count the days you have left, but count the days you have already succeeded. Think about how far you have come each day instead of thinking about how far you still have to go. Celebrate the discipline you have already practiced rather than dreading what still lies ahead of you.

> *Do not dwell on the difficulty of forming a new habit, but focus on the joy and freedom that will come as that habit gets ingrained in your daily routine and in your life.*

God sent Jesus to earth so that you might have abundant life and enjoy your life fully (John 10:10). He wants you to be happy. Can you say that you are enjoying your life? Or is some kind of habit that needs to be broken and replaced with a godly one keeping you from fully entering into the amazing quality of life Jesus died to give you? If so, then what are you waiting for? You've just completed almost an entire book on habits that will greatly improve your life. Remember that making or breaking a habit takes time, so every day that you keep going and keep working on godly habits will take you one day closer to a better, happier life.

Habit Builders

Like a city whose walls are broken through is a person who lacks self-control.

Proverbs 25:28

Do you not know that in a race all the runners run, but only one gets the prize? Run in such a way as to get the prize. Everyone who competes in the games goes into strict training. They do it to get a crown that will not last, but we do it to get a crown that will last forever.

Therefore I do not run like someone
running aimlessly; I do not fight like
a boxer beating the air. No, I strike a blow
to my body and make it my slave so that
after I have preached to others, I myself
will not be disqualified for the prize.

1 Corinthians 9:24–27

And have you completely forgotten this
word of encouragement that addresses
you as a father addresses his son?
It says, "My son, do not make light of
the Lord's discipline, and do not lose
heart when he rebukes you, because the
Lord disciplines the one he loves, and he
chastens everyone he accepts as his son."

Hebrews 12:5–6

CHAPTER 25

Eight Practical Ways to Develop Godly Habits

You'll never change your life until you change something you do daily. The secret of your success is found in your daily routine.

—John C. Maxwell

The more you develop the habits of a godly woman, the more you can look forward to the future with hope and confident expectation of good things. As you work to develop good habits with God's help, every day can be an adventure in progress rather than another day wasted doing the same old things. Every godly habit you develop will make your life better and make you happier.

In my life, I have found that I tend to slide backward if I do not take action to move forward. Life does not remain stagnant for long. Even when it may seem that nothing is happening, God is always moving, and so is the enemy. We can choose to move in God's direction or allow ourselves to be pulled in the enemy's direction.

God loves you and has an amazing plan for your life, a plan the enemy seeks to prevent from happening. God has a life of joy and purpose for you, a life the enemy seeks to steal, kill, and destroy (John 10:10). You will go far with God and in life, while disrupting the enemy's schemes, if you develop the habits that characterize a godly woman.

I am thankful that you have read this book all the way to the end, but simply reading it is not enough, nor is simply knowing about the habits of a godly woman. Now it's time to make some lasting decisions to actually incorporate good habits into your life, to make them part of how you live every day. I pray that you are ready to do that, and I believe that as you do, you will experience greater joy, peace, love, and fulfillment than you have ever known before.

> *You will go far with God and in life, while disrupting the enemy's schemes, if you develop the habits that characterize a godly woman.*

I'd like to close this book with eight practical ways to develop godly habits. I hope you will refer to them often as you develop the habits of a godly woman that are mentioned in this book and other good habits as the Lord leads you.

1. Choose one area in which you would like to build a godly habit.

It may be an area in which you would say you don't have any habit right now. For example, you may want to develop the habit of exercising regularly, but right now you do not exercise at all. Or, you may have bad habits in a certain area and you want to break those habits and replace them with good ones. A simple example of this might be that you currently eat lots of sweets and drink lots of sugary beverages, but you want to develop the habit of eating and drinking healthily. In that case, you can break the bad habit by simply choosing something healthy. It is always better to start with one habit. Then your victory in that area will increase your faith to move on to the next good habit you want to develop.

2. Be clear and specific about the habit you want to incorporate in your life.

Once you've chosen a habit you would like to develop, be clear about what you want to accomplish. Part of that clarity will come as you think and pray about your new habit and as you are specific about it. For example, you could decide that you want to develop the habit of spiritual growth. That would be wonderful, but it's a bit difficult to track. Instead you might say, "I want to grow spiritually by reordering my morning routine so I can spend more time with God in prayer before I start my day," or "I'm committed to growing spiritually by studying my Bible each day and actively participating in the weekly Bible study at church."

3. Align your thoughts and words with the godly habit you want to produce.

Thoughts and words have amazing power to produce results in our lives. When we think and speak according to God's Word, wonderful things happen. Proverbs 23:7 says that we become what we think about, and Proverbs 18:21 says, "The tongue has the power of life and death." I have done a lot of teaching on these verses in the course of my ministry, and I cannot overestimate the importance and power of their principles. When we align our thinking and our speaking with what God says and with the ways He is working in our lives, we put ourselves into agreement with Him and position ourselves to experience what we are believing Him to do. For example, if you want to develop the habit of forgiveness, a great way to move in that direction is to think and say often, "I am becoming a more forgiving person every day."

4. Be prayerful about developing new habits.

I hope you always remember that you can pray about anything. Nothing is too small or too insignificant for God; He cares about every aspect of your life. A new habit you'd like to develop doesn't have to be considered spiritual, such as studying the Bible more or praying more, for God to care about it. He is interested in anything that will help you enjoy a better life. As you're working godly habits into your life, I encourage you to undergird them with prayer, asking God for His help and wisdom to help you establish them in the ways He thinks are best for you.

5. Focus on developing a godly habit, not breaking a bad habit.

You always have a choice when you think about what to focus on. You can focus on something positive or on something negative. Romans 12:21 says that we overcome evil with good. This is true in every area of life. When we want to replace a bad habit with a good one, we can spend our energy trying to break the bad one or trying to build the good one. For example, if a person is trying to break the habit of complaining, she can focus on the fact that she complained about her boss twice in one day or on the fact that she stopped herself from complaining once that day. Focusing on the positive aspects of a situation will cause positivity to grow and keep you motivated to develop good habits.

6. Find a support system.

No matter what you do, it's easier when you have a system of support. In terms of developing godly habits, that support system could be a group of people who will encourage you and who will gently let you know if you are reverting to old ways instead of walking in new ways. It might also be some kind of app on your phone, if that's appropriate for the habit you're trying to build, or little notes in strategic places around your home or office that remind you to do things that will help you grow in your new habit. In addition, as believers, we always have the Holy Spirit, who strengthens us and helps us. Anytime you seek to develop a new habit, He is there to help you.

7. Give yourself time.

If you want to do something different in your life, you may be able to do it for a day or two, but then most people default to their old ways. Truly building a godly habit that will become part of your life for the rest of your life may require changes to your current lifestyle, and it will likely take time and energy. You can easily become overwhelmed and then want to give up if you try to tackle too many at once. The best approach is to take one day at a time, realizing that lasting change almost never happens quickly. Don't expect to build a new, godly habit instantly. Be prepared to commit to a process that will last a lifetime.

8. Celebrate the positive steps along the way.

Developing a godly habit is a process that takes time. If you are like most people, you will not establish a new habit without making a few mistakes along the way or without falling back into old patterns on occasion. It's important to keep moving forward, even when you feel you've taken a step backward. Don't let mistakes stop you or even slow you down. Keep moving toward the habit you are committed to establishing, and celebrate each step in the right direction. You may be tempted not to acknowledge your progress until you feel you've arrived, but resist it. Instead, rejoice in milestones as you reach them. For example, you may work on developing a habit of generosity and realize that for three days in a row, you have done something to serve a family member or co-worker. That's a reason to celebrate. In addition, always remember to thank God for your successes because you could not have done it without Him.

* * *

I am filled with hope as I think about the ways your life will change as you develop the habits of a godly woman. At times, the process may not be easy, but I know that with God's help, you can do it. I believe that all the habits I have written about in this book are beautiful ones to develop in your life. They will make you more like Jesus and help you represent Him better as you go through life. I encourage you to work with the Holy Spirit in developing these habits and any other habits that God impresses upon your heart.

Recently I was encouraged by the Holy Spirit to form a habit of never criticizing anyone. I would not have even considered myself a critical person, but as God opened my eyes, I saw that I had lots of room for improvement. I really enjoy growing in God and I believe that you do also.

Let's pray that God will guide us on our journey of spiritual maturity and developing the habits of a godly woman.

About the Author

Joyce Meyer is one of the world's leading practical Bible teachers. A *New York Times* bestselling author, Joyce's books have helped millions of people find hope and restoration through Jesus Christ. Joyce's program, *Enjoying Everyday Life* airs around the world on television, radio, and the Internet. Through Joyce Meyer Ministries, Joyce teaches internationally on a number of topics with a particular focus on how the Word of God applies to our everyday lives. Her candid communication style allows her to share openly and practically about her experiences so others can apply what she has learned to their lives.

Joyce has authored more than one hundred books, which have been translated into more than one hundred languages, and over

65 million of her books have been distributed worldwide. Bestsellers include *Power Thoughts*; *The Confident Woman*; *Look Great, Feel Great*; *Starting Your Day Right*; *Ending Your Day Right*; *Approval Addiction*; *How to Hear from God*; *Beauty for Ashes*; and *Battlefield of the Mind*.

Joyce's passion to help hurting people is foundational to the vision of Hand of Hope, the missions arm of Joyce Meyer Ministries. Hand of Hope provides worldwide humanitarian outreach such as feeding programs, medical care, orphanages, disaster response, human trafficking intervention and rehabilitation, and much more—always sharing the love and gospel of Christ.

JOYCE MEYER MINISTRIES

U.S. & FOREIGN OFFICE ADDRESSES

Joyce Meyer Ministries
P.O. Box 655
Fenton, MO 63026
USA
(636) 349-0303

Joyce Meyer Ministries—
Canada
P.O. Box 7700
Vancouver, BC V6B 4E2
Canada
(800) 868-1002

Joyce Meyer Ministries—
Australia
Locked Bag 77
Mansfield Delivery Centre
Queensland 4122
Australia
(07) 3349 1200

Joyce Meyer Ministries—
England
P.O. Box 1549
Windsor SL4 1GT
United Kingdom
01753 831102

Joyce Meyer Ministries—
South Africa
P.O. Box 5
Cape Town 8000
South Africa
(27) 21-701-1056

Other Books by Joyce Meyer

Joyce Meyer Spanish Titles

Books by Dave Meyer

*Study Guide available for this title

Do you have a real relationship with Jesus?

God loves you! He created you to be a special, unique, one-of-a-kind individual, and He has a specific purpose and plan for your life. And through a personal relationship with your Creator—God—you can discover a way of life that will truly satisfy your soul.

No matter who you are, what you've done, or where you are in your life right now, God's love and grace are greater than your sin—your mistakes. Jesus willingly gave His life so you can receive forgiveness from God and have new life in Him. He's just waiting for you to invite Him to be your Savior and Lord.

If you are ready to commit your life to Jesus and follow Him, all you have to do is ask Him to forgive your sins and give you a fresh start in the life you are meant to live. Begin by praying this prayer . . .

Lord Jesus, thank You for giving Your life
for me and forgiving me of my sins so I can have
a personal relationship with You. I am sincerely
sorry for the mistakes I've made, and I know
I need You to help me live right.

Your Word says in Romans 10:9, "If you declare with your mouth, 'Jesus is Lord,' and believe in your heart that God raised him from the dead, you will be saved" (NIV). *I believe You are the Son of God and confess You as my Savior and Lord. Take me just as I am, and work in my heart, making me the person You want me to be. I want to live for You, Jesus, and I am so grateful that You are giving me a fresh start in my new life with You today.*

I love You, Jesus!

It's so amazing to know that God loves us so much! He wants to have a deep, intimate relationship with us that grows every day as we spend time with Him in prayer and Bible study. And we want to encourage you in your new life in Christ.

Please visit joycemeyer.org/salvation to request Joyce's book *A New Way of Living*, which is our gift to you. We also have other free resources online to help you make progress in pursuing everything God has for you.

Congratulations on your fresh start in your life in Christ! We hope to hear from you soon.